YO-BQQ-747

SIGILLVM · BARNARDI · COLLEGII · NOVI · EBORACI ·

BARNARD COLLEGE
THE WOLLMAN LIBRARY

· MDCCCLXXXIX ·

Withdrawn from
Barnard College
Library

Jobs Your Mother Never Wanted You to Have
An Alternative Career Guide

by Carolina Vegas Starr

Loompanics Unlimited
Port Townsend, Washington

Neither the author nor the publisher assumes any responsibility for the use or misuse of information contained in this book. It is sold for informational purposes only. Be Warned!

Jobs Your Mother Never Wanted You to Have
An Alternative Career Guide
© 2003 by Carolina Vegas Starr

All rights reserved. No part of this book may be reproduced or stored in any form whatsoever without the prior written consent of the publisher. Reviews may quote brief passages without the written consent of the publisher as long as proper credit is given.

Published by:
Loompanics Unlimited
PO Box 1197
Port Townsend, WA 98368
Loompanics Unlimited is a division of Loompanics Enterprises, Inc.
Phone: 360-385-2230
E-mail: service@loompanics.com
Web site: www.loompanics.com

Cover Artwork by Craig Howell, Cheeba Productions

ISBN 1-55950-233-9
Library of Congress Card Catalog Number 2002113167

This book is dedicated to my career advisor — Lynne "The Shark" Campbell

"The return from your work must be the satisfaction which that work brings you and the world's need for that work. With this, life is heaven, or as near heaven as you can get. Without this — with work which you despise, which bores you, and which the world does not need — this life is hell."
— W.E.B. Du Bois

"Adventure, excitement, challenge, and danger combined with the possibility of a huge payday is a job description that only criminal activity can provide."
— K. Hawkeye Gross, Drug Smuggler

Contents

Introduction

"Hey, Mom, I'm a Hooker! Embalmer! Pimp! Proctologist! Worm grower! Erection shop supervisor!!!" There are some jobs you can take to earn a living — good paying jobs even — but you shouldn't be surprised when your mother doesn't brag to the neighbors about what you do. She'll lie and say you're a teacher — anything but the truth when your job title is a bit out of the ordinary. I have a female friend who is a gynecologist and her family swears she's gay and tells everyone she's a cardiologist so they don't think the same thing!!! Try to imagine what your parents would tell people if you were a cheese cutter, a jowl trimmer, or a toe puller by trade???

All jobs serve a purpose though, right? For example, where would the agriculture industry be without cabbage salters? The construction industry without breast workers? The garment industry without fingerers or fagoting machine operators? The beef industry without cowpunchers and skull grinders? And the tobacco industry without frog shakers and butt pressers??? Where, I ask, would America be without apron scratchers, bucket chunkers and mint wafer depositors?

These are all legal and legitimate occupations, but there are also many not-so-legal occupations that Americans fill every year to make a buck. Straight or off the IRS radar, the work we do is important and it impacts the entire country (sometimes even the world, as in the case of suicide bombers — not a recommended career choice!). Just think how many lunch routines would be shattered if all the bologna lacers walked off the job! Or how many members of the Partnership for a Drug-Free America would be out of work if it weren't for smack dealers.

Recently, after falling victim to a dot.com layoff, I began to think about the meaning of work and why we choose the jobs we do. Zen Buddhism teaches that the routine of work is valuable in and of itself. Whether you're a weight guesser or a Wall Street executive — it doesn't matter — a truly happy worker is one who enjoys one's work and doesn't just let one's skill set necessarily dictate one's career path. Some choose a job for the salary, some for the enjoyment, and some — like Heidi Fleiss' high-priced call girls — go for both!

So, in these unhappy economic times, would you consider changing careers to possibly find true happiness and a steady paycheck as a ladle pourer, a mangler, or an armpit sniffer? They're good jobs, but what would your parents say? Or how would the opposite sex react if you used your offbeat job title as a pick-up line? "Hey, baby, I'm a necker, but I used to be just a nibbler." "Did you know I'm a bottom buffer?" "I bet you'd never guess I'm an impregnating helper," or "Yeah, I'm a hummer operator!"

I'd have to say, the most important thing I learned from writing this book — other than discovering the broad range of career opportunities available — was where all those high school bully terms came from: "boner," "bunghole," "pile-driver," "pulverizer" — they were probably someone's dad's job!

Good luck in your job search and please note that this book is in no way an endorsement for unlawful activity; it's merely a humorous take on what you can do and what others have done — right or wrong — to make a living. It's not what you'll find on Monster.com (boring traditional stuff!) and none of the jobs in this book require advanced schooling, so there's nothing stopping you from starting your dream job immediately. But, if you decide to be a hooker, just make sure you do it in the counties in Nevada where it's legal!!!

Jobs A to Z

The Ins and Outs of Working as a Professional Accident Victim

"Thirty-five percent of Americans surveyed believe that it is all right to exaggerate insurance claims...," according to a recent Insurance Research Council (IRC) study that appeared on SmartMotorist.com. Insurance fraud is big business and the general public is cashing in!

Statistics and Your Odds of Getting Caught

The IRC study found that approximately 90 percent of the costs of insurance fraud are the result of padding claims. Claimants add damage, injuries, and fictitious passengers to their insurance claims. The other 10 percent are the result of organized accident-staging rings. Because of the sheer number of offenders, and the light sentences received by the few that are convicted, pursuing these crimes is not a priority for law-enforcement — however it *is* a goldmine for scammers! If you can lie while keeping a straight face and not feel guilty about taking advantage of others, this may be the perfect opportunity for you.

"Insurers have been making significant efforts to fight fraud," according to Elizabeth A. Sprinkel, senior vice president who heads the IRC. "While we have seen some improvement in recent years, it is still disappointing that so many Americans still see this type of insurance fraud as acceptable." Hey, everybody's doing it! It's the old "But Mom, everybody got an F" syndrome.

The overworked California Department of Insurance's Fraud Division received reports of more than 14,000 suspected fraudulent claims last year but was only able to open 300 investigations. The odds are clearly on the side of the offender.

Bumper Cars

Bumper Cars is a trend in states with no-fault insurance laws. The only thing the enterprising "victim" needs to do ahead of time is find a less than honest doctor who is willing to exaggerate or make up a false medical claim. That done, they go out and crash into someone. (They crash lightly because they don't really want to injure themselves and have to waste the insurance money on true injuries!) The no-fault insurance laws require insurers to cover anyone injured in an accident, regardless of who caused it. The accident "victim" goes to the phony doctor after the accident and has him or her file a claim. "Victims" usually end up splitting the claim 50/50 with the doctor, although in many cases the doctors receive a larger share because of their greater risk.

The Paper Accident

Over the past several years, there has been a noticeable shift from staged collisions to paper accidents. Organized criminal rings actively solicit others in the auto repair and salvage community to participate in the creation of accidents that only exist on paper. Shady lawyers, doctors, and insurance agents are often involved as well. No innocent parties are involved in this type of staged accident, because no accident ever takes place. Many insurance companies do not send investigators to examine insured vehicles when the repair bill is less than

$1,000, so this type of scam is increasing in popularity. Since the risks are small, and no police are involved, it's the easiest type of insurance fraud to commit.

The Hit and Run

This is a variation of the paper accident, is usually committed by a lone criminal and actually involves the police. If someone owns a previously damaged car and they want to get it fixed for free or close to it, they'll call the police and claim to be the victim of a hit-and-run accident, then use the report generated by the investigating officer to file a new insurance claim. Another variation is when someone is involved in an unobserved single-car accident and alleges that the accident was caused by a fictitious hit-and-run driver and give false testimony to the investigating officer.

The Swoop and Squat

Example: You're working your way through traffic on a busy four-lane thoroughfare and you're just beginning to pick up speed when all of a sudden a car cuts in front of you and slams on its brakes. Your immediate instinct is to hit the brake pedal and swerve out of the lane, but there are cars on both sides of you and there's nowhere to go. Your car smashes into the rear-end of the car that cut in front of you.

The example above was no accident. It was a staged event called a "Swoop and Squat," where the perpetrator intentionally "swoops" in front of your car and then "squats" or stops abruptly. Often an accomplice will help box you in so that you can't change lanes and avoid rear-ending the vehicle in front of you. When the police arrive, the driver and passengers of the squat car will all claim they are injured. Their claims will be validated later on by a doctor or nurse practitioner who is in on the scam and files a fraudulent medical report with your insurance company. Additionally, well-organized rings can arrange for their body shop's tow-truck to conveniently arrive on the scene before the police have time to call a legitimate one.

The Sideswipe

The Sideswipe is popular because many motorists unintentionally drift out of their lanes, or in many cases, become frustrated when they can't get out of the lane they are in and into the lane they want to be in. In a later scenario, the motorist is likely to take chances and that's where the professional accident victim comes in — speeding up to take advantage of the motorists carelessness.

This works best the more lanes there are (a busy intersection), and if the professional accident victims repeat a left turn over and over — sooner or later someone will hit them after unintentionally drifting into their lane (no signal, no checking their blind spot, or signaling, and switching lanes without looking). The point isn't necessarily to "repeat left-hand turns" as much as it is to just "stay in the same lane repeatedly until an accident occurs."

The T-bone

Here someone waits at an intersection for a lone target car to cross in front of them without any hostile witnesses. Then they'll intentionally drive into the side of the car crossing in front of them. When the police arrive, bogus witnesses that have been planted in advance claim that the target car ran a red light or a stop sign.

The Wave

This drive-down accident can happen wherever traffic is merging. The perpetrator will wave to their victim, pretending to yield the right of way. When the victim begins to merge, the waver will accelerate into the side of the victim's car (much like the sideswipe scheme). When the police arrive, they simply deny ever waving to the victim. Because the victim did not have the right of way, they're legally at fault.

In conclusion, if anyone decides to go this route (no pun intended!) — there are many options to choose from. Working independently, with a couple of friends, or finding a good seedy doctor or lawyer can get one in with a pro accident ring. Perks of this career choice, aside from the money, are that someone only need to work about 10 minutes a year to earn enough to live on.

Building the Perfect **Anarchist** Portfolio

It's important not to confuse an anarchist with a terrorist. An anarchist opposes authority while a terrorist uses threats, intimidation and destruction for political purposes. Although an anarchist's actions can be destructive and sometimes politically motivated, an anarchist's actions are usually not meant to harm and are usually just for shock value. For example, as an anarchist one might find employment with an activist group with duties that may entail setting off a smoke bomb in front of a local slaughterhouse. This would be only to draw attention to the slaughterhouse and the issues of the activist group, not to destroy the slaughterhouse or anyone else in the process. An anarchist may also find employment with a local security office or weapons maker to test their effectiveness and uncover any tampering issues the manufacturer may have overlooked.

Interview Tips

Here's one chance to impress a prospective employer by wearing jeans — that's right, leave the tie and pantsuit behind!

I recommend Dickies for the extra pockets (they'll admire your forward-thinking in planning for carrying multiple anarchist trade tools), and Dickies are a sensible buy at less than $20 at your local Wal*Mart store.

When you get that dumb, "What CD is in your player right now?" interview question, you no longer have to lie and tone down your interests by succumbing to that latest top 40. Rage Against the Machine, Marilyn Manson and Hatebreed are all acceptable answers.

Impromptu Weapons
(There are more uses for a beer can than you think)

You'll knock their socks off with your ability to transform mere trash into viable weapons within seconds. Take an ordinary beer can, soda can, and a can opener. With the can opener, fray the two ends of the can outward into a maze of jagged points. Next, tape the center section with electrical tape to form a good grip. When you swing it back and forth, you better believe it's an effective weapon.

Smoke Bombs

Here's a way to demonstrate your creative side. Smoke bombs are typically used for creating confusion and chaos or smoking someone out of a hiding area. You can easily spice up any explosive for a different effect. See the smoke screen formulas in the chart on the next page.

Numbers = % ratio based on a sum of 100. Percentage parts based on weight, not volume.

Black Smoke Screen		White Smoke Screen		Red Smoke Screen	
Magnesium Powder	19	Potassium Chlorate	44	Potassium Chlorate	20
Hexachloroethane	60	Sulfur Flour	15	Lactose	20
Naphthalene	21	Zinc Dust	40	Paranitraniline Red	60
		Sodium Bicarbonate	1		
Magnesium Powder	20	Zinc Dust	28	Potassium Chlorate	26
Hexachloroethane	60	Zinc Oxide	22	Diethylaminorosindone	
Naphthalene	20	Hexachloroethane	50		48
				Powdered Sugar	26
Hexachloroethane	55.8	Zinc Dust	66.67	Potassium Chlorate	27.4
Alpha Naphol	14	Hexachloroethane	33.33	Methylaminoanthraquin-	
Anthracene	4.6			one	42.5
Aluminum Powder	9.3			Sodium Bicarbonate	19.5
Smokeless Powder	14			Sulfur Flour	10.6
Napthalene	2.3				
Black Powder FFF	50			Potassium Perchlorate	25
Potassium Nitrate	10			Antimony Sulfide	20
Coal Tar	20			Rhodamine Red	50
Powdered Charcoal	15			Dextrin	5
Paraffin	5				

The Classic Molotov Cocktail

Happy hours are a great way to network, so know your drinks! A Molotov cocktail is an incendiary bomb, which bursts into flame upon breaking. A quart bottle is filled with two-thirds gasoline and one-third oil. The fuse from a gasoline-soaked rag is then stuffed in the mouth of the bottle. The bottle is then corked, and the fuse is lit. The Molotov cocktail is then thrown, and when it breaks, it erupts in flames. Its fire cannot be extinguished with water. According to reports, a Molotov cocktail is so powerful it can disable a tank!

Animal Eviscerator

Not a pet lover — the animal eviscerator eviscerates cattle, hogs, lambs, and small animals while performing any combination of the following tasks: slitting the body cavities of carcasses and reaching inside the abdominal cavity to cut the membranes holding the intestines. The animal eviscerator then pulls the intestines out, trims off the fat, patches leaks in the intestines using a skewer, and then places the final product on a gut truck or conveyor belt to be disposed of or to be used in by-products.

Other duties an animal eviscerator performs include: inserting a spiral rod in the gullet to sever the gullet and windpipe from other neck tissues, cutting bungs from the intestines and tying the intestines, bladder, bung, and gullet to prevent leakage, cutting out glands, ovaries, sweetbreads, liver, heart, lungs, kidneys, spleen, and spermatic cord, and placing them in containers and then on a conveyor. Additional duties include cutting bruises, blemishes, and ragged tissue from carcasses, cutting the skin from tail to shoulders to bisect carcasses and severing the heads from carcasses. The animal eviscerator may wash the viscera and carcass by using a hose, or break and bind the hoofs of lambs or sheep.

Find employment in this job by searching your local newspaper 📰, telephone book ☎, or the Web 💻 under: Beef, Butchers, Farms, Livestock Dealers, Meat Markets, Meat Packers, Meat Wholesale, Slaughterhouses.

Antisqueak Applier

An antisqueak applier applies a liquid coating to shoe parts, or cements the cushioning material between parts, to prevent squeaking from friction or wear. The antisqueak applier also brushes a coating of liquid chalk, paraffin, or wax on shoe parts, such as heels and outsoles.

Find employment in this job by searching your local newspaper 📰, telephone book ☎, or the Web 💻 under: Shoe Repair, Shoe Technicians, Shoes Retail, Shoes – Wholesale and Manufacturers.

Apron Scratcher

An apron scratcher cleans dirt and foreign matter from carded asbestos fibers, using a wire-studded scratchboard.

Find employment in this job by searching your local newspaper 📰, telephone book ☎, or the Web 💻 under: Cleaners, Clothing-Resale, Dry Cleaners, Fabric Treatment, Food Service Management, Uniforms.

Armpit Sniffer
(Someone has got to do it!)

The pharmaceutical industry is booming and forecasts project this will continue for years to come. Beta testing for personal hygiene products is essential to ensure customer satisfaction. Deodorant and antiperspirants are big business and without beta testing, these products would never make it to the shelves. Many times interns are assigned to tackle the task, but with so many brands out there, there just aren't enough interns to cover it and many companies hire from the outside.

An armpit sniffer, in a room with a controlled environment, sniffs the pits of subjects and logs an odor rating. This process is repeated with each change in temperature and with the final information, the testers can determine how effective the product is at various temperatures.

Find employment in this job by searching your local newspaper 📧, telephone book ☎, or the Web 🖥 under: Pharmaceutical Beta Testing, Pharmaceutical Consultants, Pharmaceutical Internships, Pharmaceutical Products-Wholesale and Manufacturers, Pharmaceutical Research.

Back Washer

An Italian man, a hairy back, and an employee armed with nothing more than an SOS pad ...no, that's not it!

A back washer washes, rinses, and dries silver to remove impurities, excess dyes, and odors. The back washer places balls of silver at the feed-end of a machine that draws the silver through washing and rinsing solutions, squeeze rollers, and drying cabinets. The back washer turns valves to regulate the circulation of the washing and rinsing solutions and to adjust the temperature of the drying cabinets. When complete, the back washer intermingles broken ends of fibers to piece up broken silver, may insert the ends of the silver in a gilling attachment that blends strands and winds the silver into a ball, or may weigh and pack balls of silver for shipment. The back washer may also operate a machine with an oil spray attachment that conditions fibers for further processing.

Find employment in this job by searching your local newspaper 📧, telephone book ☎, or the Web 🖥 under: Metal Cleaning, Silversmiths, Silverware, Silverware-Clean, Repair and Replate.

Bed Operator

A bed operator, contrary to popular opinion, isn't the most sexually experienced man or woman in your town. A bed operator moves rolled steel shapes, such as blooms, billets, rails, and pipe from processing lines onto cooling beds. The bed operator controls the levels to raise a roll stop, start a conveyor, and position materials opposite the specified cooling bed. He or she pulls the levers to start the pusher straightedge and dog-chain (series of projections) that shove materials off the conveyor line onto a cooling bed. He or she then moves the controls of the dog-chain to pull cooled material from the beds onto a cradle or transfer car. A bed operator also records the number and types of objects cooled and may assist other workers in making steel rolls and hot saw blade changes and in repairing, replacing, or adjusting mill equipment.

Find employment in this job by searching your local newspaper 🖥, telephone book ☎, or the Web 💻 under: Steel-Bar, Sheet, Strip and Tube, Steel Detailers-Structural, Steel Distributors and Warehouses, Steel Erectors, Steel Fabricators, Steel Stainless, Steel Structural.

Blower

Although the term is used as a slang to identify a prostitute specializing in oral sex, what a professional blower really does is insulate buildings and railway cars by blowing insulating material into spaces within walls, floors, and ceilings, using a hose attached to a blower. The blower inserts the nozzle of the hose through an opening into the spaces to be filled, turns the valve to regulate insulation flow from the hose nozzle, and moves the hose to distribute the insulating material evenly, and, when required, climbs a ladder or erects a scaffold to reach his or her working position. The blower also seals the insulation access holes with wooden bungs or metal caps using a hammer and punch and may insulate walls by covering them with sheets of insulating material, using nails or a lacing wire.

Find employment in this job by searching your local newspaper 📰, telephone book ☎, or the Web 💻 under: Insulation, Insulation Contractors, Insulation Contractors Equipment and Supplies, Insulation Materials.

Boner

As far as I know, you can't make money by simply displaying an unsightly bulge, although you may attract a lot of attention to your resume!

Type 1: This boner inserts stays (bone or steel) into prepared pockets of women's foundation garments, such as corsets or brassieres, or into casings of surgical appliances. The boner first selects the number and size of stays to be inserted and pushes them into pockets or casings by hand or by using a metal punch. Sometimes the boner may mark the insertion point, using a pencil and template, before inserting the stays. Other boner duties include cutting excess leather, cloth, and threads from appliances by using scissors, and inspecting for sewing defects.

Type 2: This boner removes bones from standard cuts of meat, such as chucks, hams, loins, plates, rounds, and shanks, to prepare the meat for packing and marketing by using a knife and a meat hook. The boner inserts a knife into the meat around bones to separate the bones from meat, fat, or tissue, then pulls and twists bones loose from the meat. The boner cuts and trims such meat cuts as butts, hams, flanks, and shoulders to shape meat and remove fat and defects, and trims meat from bones and ribs. The boner may also pull bones and skin from cooked pigs feet, and cut out toe bones and nails.

Find employment in *Type 1* boner jobs by searching your local newspaper 📰, telephone book ☎, or the Web 💻 under: Bras, Corsets and Girdles, Cloth Cutting, Clothing-Adaptive, Clothing-Women's and Misses—Wholesale and Manufacturers, Surgical Appliances, Surgical Supplies.

For *Type 2* boner jobs see animal eviscerator employment.

Bottom Buffer

A bottom buffer uses a power-driven wire brush to polish the bottoms of metal dry-cell battery containers. The bottom buffer dumps a box of containers into a tray on the bed of a machine and presses the containers into a tray to level the bottoms. He or she then starts the power-driven rotating wire brush and grasps handles on the tray and slides the tray back and forth to bring the bottoms into contact with the brush. When done, the bottom buffer inspects the can bottoms to ensure cleanliness and then withdraws the tray and inverts it over the box to return the containers.

Find employment in this job by searching your local newspaper 📰, telephone book ☎, or the Web 💻 under: Batteries-Storage-Retail, Batteries-Storage-Wholesale and Manufacturers, Battery Charging Equipment.

Bottom Hole Pressure Operator

A bottom hole pressure operator unloads recording equipment at a well site for use in determining the pressure in oil or gas wells. The bottom hole pressure operator attaches a conductor cable to an instrument and tightens clamps, fittings, and electrical connections by using wrenches and screwdrivers. The bottom hole pressure operator observes the coiling of conductor cables on the hoist drum to ensure no damage occurs to the cable and then dismantles equipment after use.

Find employment in this job by searching your local newspaper 📰, telephone book ☎, or the Web 💻 under: Contractors, Well Contractors, Wells.

Bucket Chunker

A bucket chunker is safe to invite to any party and won't vomit on your carpet! A bucket chunker smooths the inside surfaces of buckets. The bucket chunker starts by placing a bucket in the chuck of a machine by using an iron bar. The bucket chunker then steps on the pedal that starts the chuck and the bucket rotating. Next, he or she feeds a cutting tool into the inner surface of the bucket, manually smoothing the bucket, cuts the croze near the bottom of the bucket with a special attachment to the machine and rubs the top edge of the bucket with sandpaper to smooth the bucket. When finished, the bucket chunker removes the bucket from the lathe.

Find employment in this job by searching your local newspaper 📰, telephone book ☎, or the Web 💻 under:

Building Materials-Retail, Building Materials-Wholesale and Manufacturers, Contractors-Equipment and Sales, Contractors-Equipment and Sales-Renting, Contractors-Equipment and Sales-Repairing, Garden Equipment and Sales, Landscaping Equipment and Sales.

Bunghole Driver

A bunghole driver covers the bunghole of a barrel with a burlap cloth and hammers the bung and the cloth into the hole to prevent dirt from entering the barrel before it is filled.

Find employment in this job by searching your local newspaper 📧, telephone book ☎, or the Web 💻 under: Barrels and Drums.

Car Chaser

A car chaser directs the movement of grain-freight cars in a plant yard and selects the cars for grain loading. The car chaser signals railroad crews and plant workers to move cars in a specified sequence to meet grain loading and unloading schedules, marks or points out cars for use and walks along the railroad tracks to examine empty grain cars to ascertain size, type, and cleanliness. The car chaser is also responsible for selecting cars for future loading and preparing lists of the car numbers.

Find employment in this job by searching your local newspaper 📧, telephone book ☎, or the Web 💻 under: Farming Equipment, Feed Dealers, Freight Forwarding.

Carcass Splitter

A carcass splitter performs any combination of tasks involved in dismembering and cutting up hog, veal, beef, and other animal carcasses to facilitate handling preparatory to marketing or further processing. The carcass splitter uses knifes, cleavers, hand and power saws, and other cutting tools. The carcass splitter saws or cuts through the pelvic area of an animal, and splits the belly to expose and remove viscera, splits the suspended carcass in half lengthwise along the backbone of beef sides, and smoothes and shapes the beef with a paddle, saws ribs along the interior of hog carcasses to facilitate removal of loins and ribs, and cuts, cleaves, or saws carcass sections to sever forequarters, hindquarters, shoulders, rumps, legs, and other parts. The carcass splitter also saws trimmed bones, such as skulls, ribs, and legs, into pieces preparatory to processing into byproducts and may also be employed as a rump sawyer.

Find employment in this job by searching your local newspaper 📰, telephone book ☎, or the Web 💻 under: Beef, Butchers, Farms, Livestock Dealers, Meat Markets, Meat Packers, Meat Wholesale, Slaughterhouses.

Catch Can Man

The catch can man, sometimes called the "Most Important Job in NASCAR!," is responsible for catching any overflow of fuel when race cars are gassing up in the pits. The catch can man applies a special container to the overflow vent of a race car in order to gather any gas that flows back from the car's fuel tank. The catch can man, in order to catch any fuel spurts, then follows the race car for a few yards as it leaves the pit and accelerates.

Find employment in this job by searching your local newspaper 📰, telephone book ☎, or the Web 💻 under: Auto Racing, NASCAR, Pit Crews.

Cheese Cutter

A cheese cutter typically passes gas, but when you're paid to do it, it involves cutting blocks of cheese into pieces of a specified shape and size. The cheese cutter examines cheese for defects in color, texture, and body. The cheese cutter begins by bolting a specified cutting head to a machine using a wrench, adjusting stops on the cutting table, and turning the necessary wheels to position the cutting wires. Once the equipment is set, the cheese cutter places cheese blocks on the table and moves the lever to lower the cutting head or to raise the table to cut cheese. Other duties may include weighing the cut cheese, placing cheese pieces on a conveyor, and recording the amount of cheese cut. The cheese cutter may also measure cheese with a ruler and cut it with a hand cutter if need be, or trim the rind, mold, or sediment from the cheese using a knife.

Find employment in this job by searching your local newspaper 📰, telephone book ☎, or the Web 💻 under: Cheese, Dairies, Dairy Products-Retail, Dairy Products-Wholesale, Food Processing, Foods-Ready to Serve.

Chick Sexer

A chick sexer examines a chick's genitalia to determine its sex. To do this, the chick sexer turns back the skin fold of the external cloacal opening or inserts an illuminating viewer into the cloaca to observe genitals. Once the sex is determined, the chick sexer places the chicks into boxes according to sex and marks content data on the boxes of segregated chicks.

Find employment in this job by searching your local newspaper, telephone book, or the Web under: Farms, Poultry Farms, Poultry-Wholesale.

Corduroy Brusher

A corduroy brusher pushes a truck or roll of cloth into a feeding position, then sews the ends of the cloth to the leader in a machine equipped with a series of brushing units by using a portable sewing machine. Next, the corduroy brusher turns the crank to set the width guides according to the size of the cloth. When ready, the corduroy brusher starts the machine and observes the cloth to detect grease spots, holes, or torn selvages as the cloth is drawn between rollers and brushes, and turns a valve to admit water into the trough of the wet brushing unit. Lastly, he or she may move the cloth from the swing-folding attachment onto a hand-truck.

Find employment in this job by searching your local newspaper, telephone book, or the Web under: Cleaners, Clothing-Resale, Dry Cleaners, Fabric Shops, Fabric Treatment, Fabric-Wholesale and Manufacturers.

Corn Popper

A corn popper lights one or more ovens and starts rotating a cone- or drum-shaped, perforated oven before dumping a measured amount of corn into the oven. The corn popper then places a container at the discharge end of the oven to receive the popcorn and starts the conveyor to carry corn through a screen to remove unpopped kernels. The corn popper moves a lever to reverse the rotation of the oven and to dump those unpopped kernels into another container beneath the oven. When popping corn by the wet method, the corn popper pushes a lever to release a measured amount of oil onto unpopped corn in a stationary oven. Other duties may include preparing syrup and coating to make popcorn candy or other popcorn products.

Find employment in this job by searching your local newspaper 📰, telephone book ☎, or the Web 💻 under: Food Processing, Foods-Ready to Serve, Popcorn Products-Manufacturers.

Cowpuncher

Jobs in the Wild, Wild West are far from extinct, so grab your spurs if wranglin' is your dream. A cowpuncher, sometimes referred to as a cowboy, performs any combination of the following duties on a beef cattle ranch: herding, castrating, and branding cattle; inspecting and repairing fences, windmills, watering troughs, and feed containers; feeding cattle supplemental food during shortages of natural forage. The cowpuncher may also train saddle horses and ride beside horses being trained to prevent the horse from bucking or the rider from being injured. Although the *Job Almanac* recently rated this job one of the least desirable due to its physicality, the beef industry continues to thrive regardless of the popularity of vegetarianism. If lassoing and the great outdoors interest you, this may be the perfect job match.

(i)—Find employment in this job by searching your local newspaper 📰, telephone book ☎, or the Web 💻 under: Farms, Fence Repair, Livestock Dealers.

Crime and Trauma Scene Clean-Up for Beginners

It's a pretty sick job, but if no one cleaned up after car accidents and other deadly occurrences, could you imagine what our streets would look like? Or what you'd be in store for if you answered a classified for an "unfurnished apartment?"

Crime and trauma scene workers handle homicides, suicides, all types of accidents (car, construction, you name it!) and decompositions. They not only remove body parts, but are also responsible for packaging and disposing of all biohazardous waste found at the scene, i.e., blood, human excrement, and tissue. And, odor elimination is just par for the course in this job.

Basic carpentry and construction skills can get you into some of the more elite crime and trauma scene cleaning companies, with services extending to drywalling, painting, restoration, and structural repair.

In order to work as a crime and trauma scene worker, you need to have all the necessary vaccinations as well as basic blood borne pathogen training, which teaches about the potentially harmful residue found at crime and trauma scenes and the possible transmission of harmful pathogens (microorganisms). The typical biohazard equipment you'll need for the job include:

- Disposable latex gloves
- Disposable footwear protectors (booties)
- Disposable face mask/shield
- Disposable gown/apron
- Disposable biohazardous waste bag (trash)

Freelancing positions in this field are available. Call your neighborhood funeral home or...

(i) Find employment in this job by searching your local newspaper 📧, telephone book ☎, or the Web 💻 under: Crime and Trauma Scene clean-up.

How to Form and Reap the Benefits of Your Own Cult

They are charismatic and the true bad boys. The media and the "Movie of the Week" makers love them! They are cult leaders — the ultimate Micro Managers with a recipe for success.

Jim Jones in 1957, after raising cash by selling South American monkeys door-to-door, hung a shingle announcing the "People's Temple" outside a rented storefront in Indianapolis. The population in the area was rapidly changing from white to black. Jim Jones found a niche market and was ready to cash in on it.

Jim Jones, using a bag of gimmicks and public relations tricks (such as paying off parishioners to fake illnesses so he could pretend to heal them) attracted crowds of curiosity-seekers and with the curiosity-seekers came donations. The People's Temple defined itself as an urban Christian mission, a place where people down on their luck and looking for comfort could find not only spiritual uplift, but also a meal, a bed, a sense of community in a rootless environment, and quite often a job. Jim Jones used the resulting pool of cheap labor to set up many small businesses in the area to channel money into his temple.

Prosperity in turn attracted even more followers, and soon the temple was a big business that boasted a hundred-voice choir and drew jubilant crowds to Sunday services. His growing clout was exemplified in 1961 when Jim Jones was appointed the director of the Human Rights Commission for the city — all for being nothing more than a master scammer!

With that success and the Sunday hat full of cash, Jones went all out — diamond rings, alligator shoes and travel in the style of a dignitary — and his followers were so happy to be part of a community after society at large had rejected them that they didn't question the way the money was being spent. In addition to the businesses and a growing membership, came frequent fundraising drives in which congregants were expected to show their loyalty by pledging their wages or welfare money, Social Security checks, even real estate and bank holdings.

Jim Jones found his place in history after a long reign similar to that of a rock star: sunglasses, good looks, and screaming fans. His power not only reached his followers, but grocery stores everywhere after all the members of the People's Temple committed suicide by drinking poison. Kool Aid will never be the same — now that's impact!!!

Three steps to cult leadership success can be broken down like this:

1. Find a niche
2. Understand your market
3. Own your market anyway you can

If you have a sales and marketing background, the cult business might be your next step.

Charles Manson went from two-bit thief to king of his own commune. He graced the front page of nearly every newspaper in the country and was featured on the cover of *Rolling Stone* magazine. He did it all through his power and influence over people. They gave him friendship, money, shelter, and ultimately even killed for him. In his bestseller *Helter Skelter*, Vincent Bugliosi explains how Charlie, like Jim Jones, climbed up the rungs on the ladder of success.

Those who were drawn to Charles Manson were not the typical girl or boy next door. Nearly all had within them a deep-seated hostility toward society and everything it stood for which pre-existed their meeting Manson. Those who chose to go with him did so, as Dr. Joel Hochman testified in the sensational trial, "for reasons, which lie within the individuals themselves." In short, there was a need, and Manson seemed to fulfill it. But it was a double process of selection. For Manson decided who stayed. He did not want anyone who he felt would challenge his authority, cause dissension in the group, or question his dogma. Sounds like a typical manager or supervisor, right?

Much like a corporate figurehead who uses money and position to control his or her employees, Manson capitalized on the needs of those who surrounded him. His ability to "psyche out" people was so great that many of his disciples felt he could read their minds. Having had many, many years to study human nature in prison, and being a sophisticated con man, Manson realized that there are certain problems that nearly every human being is beset with. Manson made it a point to find out what someone's problem was, and supply at least a semblance of a solution to it, whether it was a father surrogate, a Christ figure, a need for acceptance and belonging, or a leader in a leaderless time.

Drugs were another of his tools. As brought out in the psychiatric testimony during the trials, LSD was not a causal agent but a catalyst. Manson used it very effectively, to make his followers more suggestible, to implant ideas, to extract "agreements." Reportedly, Charlie always took a smaller dose than the others in order to remain in command.

Charlie used repetition. By constantly preaching and lecturing to his subjects on an almost daily basis, he was able to gradually and systematically erase their inhibitions. Manson himself once remarked in court, "You can convince anybody of anything if you just push it at them all the time. They may not believe it 100%, but they will still draw opinions from it, especially if they have no other information to draw their opinions from."

In addition to repetition, Charlie used isolation. There were no newspapers or TVs. Cut off from the rest of society, he created a timeless society of his own.

He used sex. Realizing that most people have sexual hang-ups, he taught by both precept and example, that in sex there was no wrong, thereby eradicating both their inhibitions and their guilt. But there was more than just sex, there was love. Love was one of the strongest bonds among them. The love grew out of their sharing, their communal problems and pleasures, and their relationship with Charlie. They did everything willingly for Charlie because it pleased him.

He also used fear very effectively — even to mask his own paranoia. In a *Newsweek* article, a professor from Stanford University named Philip Zimbardo, explains, "By raising the level of fear around you, your own fear seems more normal and socially acceptable."

He brought to the surface his followers' latent hatred, their inherent penchant for sadistic violence, focusing it on a common enemy, the establishment. He depersonalized their prospective victims by making them symbols.

He taught his followers a completely immoral philosophy, which provided complete justification for their acts. If everything is right, then nothing can be wrong. If nothing is real, then all life is a game. He brought them from panhandling and petty theft to prostitution and armed robbery to murder.

It makes you wonder, if he used his influence for positive means, would Charles Manson be a multimillionaire today instead of a convict? Either way, he made a thriving business out of society's rejected members. Evil or enterprising, Charles Manson achieved personal success

Dot Etcher

A dot etcher increases or reduces the size of photographic dots by chemical or photomechanical methods to make color corrections on halftone negatives or positives to be used in the preparation of lithographic printing plates. The dot etcher, using a magnifying glass or densitometer, examines film on a light table to determine the specified color and color balance. The dot etcher compares the proof print of a color separation negative or positive with the customer's original sample or a copy and a standard color chart to determine the accuracy of reproduction, identifies and marks color discrepancies on the print and film, and prepares dyes or other chemical solutions according to standard formulas and applies a solution to the inaccurately colored areas of the film to correct the color. The dot etcher blocks out or modifies color shades of the film by using a template, brushes, and opaque, and then prepares photographic masks to protect areas of the film not needing correction by using a contact frame and an automatic film processor, or by manually cutting masking material, to correct color by the photomechanical method. After determining the extent of the correction and the exposure length needed based on experience or predetermined exposure and color charts, the dot etcher places masks over separation negatives or positives and exposes film for a specified time by using a contact frame and an automatic film processor to reduce the size of photographic dots to increase or reduce color. The dot etcher also applies opaque to defective areas of film to block out blemishes and pinholes.

Find employment in this job by searching your local newspaper 📰, telephone book ☎, or the Web 🖥 under: Photo Finishing-Retail, Photo Finishing-Wholesale, Photo Laboratories-Commercial, Photo Printers, Photo Retouching and Restoration, Photographic Color Prints and Transparencies.

Drug Smuggling, The Basics

Drug smuggling *is* a very profitable business. You've seen the movies — *Scarface, Desperado, Blow* — just to name a few. Hollywood sure doesn't make big budget movies with the hottest stars about line cooks or customer service representatives!

Just How Profitable Is It? Very!

"The average drug trafficking organization, meaning from Medellin to the streets of New York, could afford to lose 90% of its profit and still be profitable," says Robert Stutman, a former DEA Agent. "Now think of the analogy. GM builds a million Chevrolets a year. Doesn't sell 900,000 of them and still comes out profitable. That is a hell of a business, man. That is the dope business."

In their article "Do the Math: Why the Illegal Drug Business Is Thriving" by Oriana Zill and Lowell Bergman, (PBS Website: *Frontline*, www.pbs.org/wgbh/pages/frontline/shows-/drugs/special/math.html) the authors explain that the single largest marketplace for illegal drugs continues to be the United States. Although the market has decreased dramatically since its heyday in the mid-80s, close to thirteen million Americans still pony up for a gram of cocaine, a few hits of Ecstasy or a quarter ounce of weed to party with their friends on the weekends. A hardcore group estimated at between 5 and 6 million have more serious drug habits, and may spend $100-$500 dollars a week on purchasing their drugs. These two groups — hardcore users and casual users — spend approximately $60 billion a year, according to U.S. government estimates.

Imagine a typical weekend in New York City. Experts estimate that at least one percent of the population — 80,000 plus — spends $200 on illicit drugs. That alone would amount to $16 million dollars a week or $832 million a year. And that's just New York City!

What keeps the drug industry going is its huge profit margins. Producing drugs is a very cheap process. As in any commodities business, location is everything! Processed cocaine is available in Colombia for $1500 per kilo and sold on the streets of America for as much as $66,000 a kilo (retail). Heroin costs $2,600/kilo in Pakistan, but can be sold on the streets of America for $130,000/kilo (retail). And synthetics like methamphetamine are often even cheaper to manufacture, costing approximately $300 to $500 per kilo to produce in clandestine labs in the U.S. and abroad and sold on U.S. streets for up to $60,000/kilo (retail).

Drug expenditures in billions of dollars.

Drug	1988	1990	1992	1994	1996	1998
Cocaine	76.9	61.3	49.4	42.2	41.3	39.0
Heroin	21.8	17.6	10.9	10.5	11.7	11.6
Marijuana	11.3	13.5	12.5	11.4	9.0	10.7
Methamphetamines	2.4	2.4	1.6	2.1	2.1	1.5
Other Drugs	3.3	2.2	1.5	2.6	2.7	2.3
TOTAL	115.7	97.0	75.9	68.6	66.8	65.0

Source: Abt Associates Inc., What America's Users Spend on Illegal Drugs, 1988-98
Amounts are in constant 1998 dollars.

Finding the Right People

Running a successful drug smuggling operation all comes down to people — finding the right people for the right jobs and doing it in a careful, back-channel way to minimize the chance of law enforcement getting involved. From source-country sellers and workers to pilots and boat captains to ground crews in the United States to vehicle drivers, safe-house babysitters, chiefs of sales, money transporters, and legal advisors, multinational drug smuggling can't be done without a lot of people being involved.

So, knowing how important choices are, here are some methods smugglers use to find the right people:

1. *Don't offer the opportunity to anyone whose presence isn't necessary for the success of the mission.*
2. *Be sure that at least one group member has known a prospective group member for a minimum of five years.*
3. *Look for relevant job skills.* People who know boats and airplanes, vehicle people, and ground-crew unloaders ful-

fill the major smuggling job classifications. Airplane pilots and mechanics, boat captains, and maintenance people are the people you're looking for.

4. *Look for combat experience.* Combat veterans know what it feels like to be scared and to press on with the mission. A smuggling run is a combat mission, and whatever his fears might be, if the vet has made the decision to smuggle he isn't going to wear his fears on his sleeve. Nothing destroys the morale and collective psyche of a smuggling group more quickly than someone's announcement of how afraid he is of getting caught right before the mission is set to launch.

   The next best thing to combat experience is military experience. The military emphasis is on teamwork, doing your job and adapting to change. These are three of the most important aspects of smuggling.

5. *A married person is less desirable than someone who is unmarried.* The less ties the better. The same rule applies to someone who is close to his or her family as opposed to someone who isn't.

6. *Avoid drug and alcohol abusers.* Someone who can't handle his liquor or drugs can bring unwanted problems to the group.

7. *Watch out for the "trickster" syndrome.* The act of smuggling drugs is illegal, but that doesn't mean you have to complicate the situation by committing a host of other illegal acts.

Finding a Source

A source is the person in the country where the drugs are who gets the load together to be smuggled into the United States. This is how a smuggler finds the right source:

1. *They don't search for the golden person in the United States.* Mexico and Jamaica are easy. They have huge

American tourist industries, and all shapes, sizes, and colors of Americans come and go, needing only proof of American citizenship. Columbia is tougher due to years of bad publicity. For the initial trip, the smuggler might find it's best to go as part of a tour group to avoid arousing any suspicion. They would find a tour in the area in which the potential smuggler is interested: in Columbia, Santa Marta or Barranquilla; in Mexico, a good starting spot is Chihuahua; in Jamaica, Montego Bay or Negril.

2. *They check into the nicest hotel, slip the bartender some cash, and indicate to him that they'd like to meet someone who can supply marijuana or cocaine in substantial weights.* This will start the ball rolling. Every big hotel or resort has a person to handle the unusual needs of the guests, and the word of what his/her needs are will get them to the right person.

   If nothing happens fast enough, just walking down the streets will bring out teenagers offering to sell dope and girls. With a word of encouragement, they'll be off to find their cousin, who is a big dealer and knows where to get big amounts. More often than not, these kids will take the few dollars given to them and disappear, but if things aren't happening yet, there isn't a whole lot to lose in seeing if they bring anyone back for a meeting.

3. *They go directly to the police or customs people.* Yes, in the United States, law-enforcement personnel are generally well paid and can't be bribed. This is definitely not the case in drug-source countries. In these countries, the police and other law enforcement agencies are on the side of the drug trade. All the smuggler needs to do is pay them to get their cooperation.

   The police don't want to deal directly with Americans, but they will certainly know a person to put the smuggler in contact with who can handle his needs and wants. The police to contact are ones in small towns. A smuggler wouldn't walk into the Montego Bay police station, but rather go to the other side of the island to Sav-la-Mar, slip a low-ranking cop some money, and tell him what they are looking for.

The three major areas a drug source is responsible for are (a.) finding the load and getting it together for shipping; (b.) finding the landing strip or dock that is going to be used for the loading and making sure all fuel and equipment are at the scene; (c.) paying off everyone who needs to be paid off. That's why the source is so important — he basically is in charge of the whole operation.

Getting Drugs Into the Country

The essence of the drug-smuggling mission comes down to one thing — getting the drug cargo into the United States. The plans and schemes to accomplish this run the gamut. People have swallowed balloons and condoms filled with cocaine, built half-mile tunnels under the Mexican-U.S. border, and liquefied cocaine to bring it in as wine. The plots, conspiracies, and schemes are endless.

That's part of the beauty of smuggling — the game constantly changes. How many straight jobs offer that as opposed to years and years of monotony? Quick adaptation ensures continued success. The trick — read and listen. Go online, watch CNN and read *High Times*. The smuggler combines information from national media with the local news in an area that will be smuggled into — they need to be well informed about current happenings. The TV shows *America's Most Wanted* and *Law & Order* keep very current with the crimes they portray and are worth checking out.

Whether smuggling is accomplished via air, land or sea, the plan for a smuggling run should be as simple as possible and as cheap as possible. Then the smuggler should compare that plan to the up-to-date information available about law enforcement activities, such as recent stings, and not mimic the plan of anyone who was busted. If the plan checks out, they proceed; if not, then back to the drawing board. A little time spent rehashing a plan is a lot better than serving a long time in prison.

Some Occupational Hazards

Communication: Smugglers use only pay phones, do not talk in public places, and confine in-person conversations to private homes and cars.

How smugglers obtain a fake ID:

1. *They buy at the Mexican-American Border.* A few hundred dollars will buy a driver's license with a photo, a Social Security card, and a birth certificate. From there they can immediately present themselves as someone else. The section of Tijuana, Nogales, or any Mexican border town where the strip joints and bars are is where they'll find the hustlers to steer them to the ID makers.

2. *They get a friend to give them his or hers.* Then the friend can report his wallet lost and have all of it reissued. The problem with this is if something bizarre happens and any kind of police pressure is applied to the friend, the friend may talk. Plus, they may not want to get their friend in trouble.

3. *Get a U.S. passport in a phony name.* This is the most effective fake ID, but one of the toughest to obtain. First step, acquire the driver's license of a person of the same sex. Usually one can bribe a bouncer or ID checker at a college bar, so that when he confiscates a fake ID, he'll pass it on. Then a PO box would be rented, using this driver's license as ID.

   Next, if a friend or relative died young, the smuggler is ahead of the game. They'll want someone around the same age. If the date and place of death is known one can get a death certificate. A death certificate is a public record, and it contains a person's full name, place of birth, date of birth, mother's maiden name and Social Security number.

The smuggler would call the county records bureau in the county where the person died to find out what is required. Most charge a small fee, ask that they state their relationship to the deceased, and require an enclosed photocopy of their driver's license — just the driver's license from the bar.

With the information from the death certificate in hand, they can then proceed to get a birth certificate. Again, a call to the county records office to ask what the requirements are for a replacement birth certificate is necessary. Most likely they will just have to send a letter stating that they need the birth certificate, plus a money order to cover costs. They would change the name on their PO box to match the name of the identity they are assuming.

To assume the identity of an unknown person they would go to the library and get back copies of the local paper or go online to search the obituaries. An obit will usually give enough information to obtain a birth certificate as previously described.

Once they have the birth certificate they're on their way to gaining quite a collection of fake IDs. If they have knowledge of a Social Security number, they could write for a replacement card. They would register to vote and receive a voter's card — or even open up a checking account!

The first picture ID one would get is a proof-of-age card that all states issue to people who don't drive. Any big-city area will suffice, in that most residents rely on public transportation. With the proof-of-age picture ID, and a PO box in the town where they will be seeking a driver's license, they're ready for the DMV.

For a driver's license, generally three kinds of ID are needed. A call ahead will ensure the smuggler has the required information and then they just need to pass the driving test.

With a birth certificate, Social Security card, a proof-of-age card from one state, a driver's license from another state, plus some assorted fill-in IDs, they're set. And, the smuggler has all the ingredients to cook up a phony passport. Passport applications can be found online — once they are filled out, mailed in, six weeks later they'll receive their passport.

Money

If all goes well with the smuggling operation the smuggler is going to have more cash around they know what to do with. Salaries or profits from illegal drug-smuggling don't come with an IRS 1099 form. This is money the government knows nothing about, and as the recipient of this unknown money, it's the smugglers job to disperse it back into the monetary system without drawing attention to himself.

For the smuggler, living "The Cash Life" revolves around the concept that there be no trace of any illegally gained money spent. That may sound simple, but it really means radically changing spending habits. This can be as hard as dieting! They have to think of money in two ways: good money and bad money. Good money is all money obtained through legal means; Bad money is all money obtained through illegal means. Bad money can't be deposited in traditional ways like in a checking or savings account.

Bad money can be used to pay, via cash or money order, for every aspect of the smuggler's life while good money collects interest! Bad money lets a person go about his or her business and takes away the one thing that law enforcement counts on the most in prosecuting drug cases: a paper trail. If a paper trail of spending can be established, then the next step — proving that a person has no visible means to pay for expenditures — becomes easy. A paper trail of expenditures and purchases proves that they cannot possibly afford the lifestyle they lead unless they are receiving unreported money. The trick — they leave no records!

Egg Foo Cash:
How to Become an Egg Donor

Infertility has become an increasingly serious problem for couples in the U.S. and Canada, while the importance of sexuality research grows steadily. Studies show that one out of every three couples are likely to face the problem of infertility and other sexual dysfunctions. What this means is that for fertile men and women there's a growing demand for services — and good compensation to boot! So, which type of egg donation is right for you?

Open Program: You and prospective parents exchange personal contact information, photographs, and possibly meet in person. The level of contact is decided by you and the prospective parent or parents. You may or may not receive information regarding the outcome of your donation, depending on what both parties decide.

Closed Program: You remain completely anonymous and no personal contact information will be exchanged. You will not receive photos, updates, or contact from the prospective parent or parents. You may or may not even receive information regarding the outcome of your donation (was it successful or not).

Flexible Program: You are willing to participate in either the Open or Closed program, whichever has the highest demand.

Egg Donor Requirements

You must be:

1. Between the ages of 18 and 32. (This can vary. Some clinics cut off donors at age 30 and some accept donors up until the age of 34.)
2. A high school graduate.
3. In good general health, disease-free, and willing to be tested accordingly.
4. Mature and responsible.
5. Available and committed to the donation process, which involves traveling to and from fertility clinics for monitoring and retrieval. You must take numerous injections on a strict schedule, as well as blood tests, ultrasounds, and undergo the retrieval procedure, which entails a needle, attached to a vaginal ultrasound device, which pierces the vaginal wall to extract the eggs.
6. You have not donated more than five times previously. (Most clinics cut off donors after the sixth time.) If you are an experienced egg donor, age limits may be extended and compensation may be increased.

Suggested fee for egg donation ranges typically from $3,500-$7,500.

In addition to the egg donor requirements stated above, you must also have at least one of the following:

- SAT score of 1150 or higher
- ACT score of 20 or higher
- IQ score of 125 or higher

and

- be enrolled in college or graduated from college with a cumulative GPA of 3.00 or higher.

Egg Donation Centers

The Center for Egg Donation
Center for Reproductive Health
Internet: www.eggdonation.net/
e-mail: drvasquez@thecenterforreproductivehealth.com
326 21st Avenue, North
Nashville, TN 37203
Phone: 615-321-8899
Fax: 615-321-8877

Conceptual Options
Internet: www.conceptualoptions.com
e-mail: maryann@conceptualoptions.com
A center for surrogacy, egg donation and embryo adoption.
10650 Treena Street, Suite 103
San Diego, CA 92131
Phone: 858-577-0358
Fax: 858-577-0355

Creating Families, Inc.
Internet: www.eggdonorfertilitybank.com
e-mail: info@eggdonor.net
Online database registry for egg donation, surrogate parent-
ing and embryo adoption.
1395 Bellaire Street
Denver, CO 80220
Phone: 303-355-2107
Fax: 303-355-1132

Donor Ovum Articles
Internet: www.ihr.com/resolve/ar-egg.html

Donor Egg Program
Genetics and IVF Institute
Internet: www.givf.com/donoregg_vx.html
e-mail: eggdonor@GIVF.com
3015 Williams Drive
Fairfax, VA 22031
Phone: 800-552-4363, 703-876-3869
Fax: 703-698-0418

Donor Oocyte Program
The Iowa Women's Health Center
Internet: www.uihc.uiowa.edu/pubinfo/arc.htm
Advanced Reproductive Care, 2 Boyd Tower
The University of Iowa Hospitals and Clinics
200 Hawkins Drive
Iowa City, IA 52242-1009
Phone: 319-356-UIVF (8483)
Fax: 319-353-6659

Egg Donor and Surrogacy Program
Internet: www.eggdonation.com
Los Angeles, CA

Family Fertility Center — Egg Donor and Surrogate Info
Internet: www.surromother.com/
e-mail: ffc@surromother.com
2855 Mitchell Drive, Suite #104
Walnut Creek, CA 94598
Phone: 510-977-4850
Fax: 510-977-4854

The Fertility Institutes — Egg Donor Profiles
Internet: www.fertility-docs.com/
18370 Burbank Blvd., Suite 414
Tarzana, CA 91356
Phone: 818-776-8700
Fax: 818-776-8754

Genesis Family Services
Egg Donation, Embryo Donation
Internet: www.GenesisFamilyServices.com/
e-mail: info@genesisfamilyservices.com
185 County Road 1801
Holly Pond, AL 35083
Phone: 888-517-8401

Logan Institute For Assisted Reproduction
Internet: www.loganinstitute.com/welcome.htm
e-mail: info@loganinstitute.com
Launching in January 2002. Aims to speed matching of donor and recipient, and help women over the age of 45
London, United Kingdom

Mothers via Egg Donation FAQ
Internet: www.surrogacy.com/online_support/mved/faq.html

Ova the Rainbow
Egg donation and surrogacy agency
Internet: ovatherainbow.homestead.com/webpage1.html
e-mail: ovatherainbow@cheerful.com
Free online egg donor database and lots of hands on service for all involved
PO Box 187
Stevinson, CA 95374
Phone: 209-669-8556
Fax: 775-307-9948

Portland Center for Reproductive Medicine
(egg donation program)
2222 NW Lovejoy, Suite 404
Portland, OR 97210
Phone: 503-274-4994
Fax: 503-274-4946

Reproductive Specialty Medical Center
Internet: www.drary.com
e-mail: info@drary.com
1441 Avocado Avenue, Suite 203
Newport Beach, CA 92660
Phone: 949-640-7200, 800-414-7299
Fax: 949-720-0203
Egg donors with photo as adults and as children, diverse choice of ethnic heritage and occupations available gestational surrogacy and donor sperm available

Sowing the seeds... Women explore their options with egg donation
Internet:
news.vpsa.asu.edu/The%20Bulldog/051398/seeds.html

Surrogate Alternatives
Internet: www.SurrogateAlternatives.com/
e-mail: SurrOption@aol.com
1995 Moss Landing Avenue
Chula Vista, CA 91913
Phone: 619-397-0757

Woman to Woman Fertility Center
Internet: www.ihr.com/woman/
e-mail: wwfc@compuserve.com
3201 Danville Boulevard, Suite 160
Alamo, CA 94507
Phone: 510-820-9495
Fax: 510-820-3885

Embalming
— The Next Big Thing!

An Embalmer's Job Description

An embalmer is a person who engages in the disinfection, preparation, preservation or restoration of human remains.

The mouth, nose and other orifices are sanitized and packed and sewn by the embalmer to prevent excretions, which could be a source of disease or infection. Embalming chemicals are then injected into the body through one or more accessible arteries, while body fluids are drained through corresponding veins.

The chemicals an embalmer uses kill bacteria and temporarily preserve the body by altering the physical structure of the body's proteins. A latticework of inert, firm protein is created that can no longer serve as a host for bacteria or be acted upon by enzymes. Thus, through embalming, the decomposition process is retarded and the body is sanitized and temporarily preserved.

The embalmer also performs cosmetic and restorative work in the process, in the event the deceased had been in an accident or has begun to decompose. Embalmers can additionally be responsible to supervise funeral attendants and other funeral home staff.

Embalmers are often required to work irregular hours. Funeral homes are usually open on evenings and weekends and, as a result, shift work is often required. Hours may vary more in smaller funeral homes, though in larger ones, employees generally work 8 hours a day for 5 or 6 days a week.

Embalmers must to be able to deal with highly emotional situations as they interact with grieving families in sensitive times. They need to know the legislation governing the handling of human remains, and have knowledge detailing the financial rules and regulations pertaining to estates of the deceased, as well as the laws pertaining to cross-border remains movement (within and outside of Canada). Embalmers must be aware of, and sensitive to, potential religious requirements. They also have to be prepared to work with the coroner and medical doctors and be aware of the potential results of contagious diseases. They sometimes are required to market funeral services and products, such as caskets.

Salary

An embalmer working full time earns an average of $33,438 per year. Wages of freelance embalmers average approximately $20 per hour. Responsible and committed embalmers increase their chances of full-time, on-going employment and career success.

Career Projections

The number of those involved in the embalming trade is officially estimated to have grown by nearly one-fifth in the last 10 years. About 15% of all embalmers are self-employed, slightly higher than the economy-wide average of 11%.

This occupation is anticipated to experience moderate growth in the near future, with more extensive growth projected in the next 10 to 15 years due to the aging of the current population. Regional differences will yield more or less opportunity in this trade depending on several variables, including the population size, dominant regional industry, recreational activities, and types of roads and traffic.

With corporations stepping in and buying up funeral homes on a regular basis, salaries, benefits and pensions for embalmers are due to become increasingly more desirable in the coming years.

The Curriculum

The following is a standard Funeral Service curriculum offered by the Simmons Institute of Funeral Service, Inc. in Syracuse, New York.

Public Health and Technical Content

	PHT 3053 - Chemistry	
	PHT 2074 - Embalming Theory	
	PHT 3134 - Restorative Art	
	PHT 4243 - Pathology	
	PHT 2001 - Practicum	
	PHT 3001 - Practicum	Hours: 16

Business Management Content

	BMC 1023 - Computer Applications	
	BMC 1093 - Accounting	
	BMC 3153 - Small Business Management	
	BMC 3172 - Funeral Directing and Professional Relationships	
	BMC 4223 - Funeral Home Administration	Hours: 14

Liberal Arts Requirements

	LAR 1003 - English Composition	
	LAR 2143 - Effective Business Communications	
	LAR 1083 - Essentials of Mathematics	
	LAR 2044 - Anatomy	
	LAR 4203 - Microbiology/Health	Hours: 16

Social Science Content

	SSC 1163 - Introduction to Psychology	
	SSC 2063 - Introduction to Sociology	
	SSC 4102 - History of Funeral Service	
	SSC 4183 - Funeral Service Counseling	Hours: 10

Legal, Regulatory, and Ethical Content

	LRE 2112 - Business Law I	
	LRE 3142 - Business Law II	
	LRE 4192 - Funeral Service Law and Ethics	Hours: 6
	Total	Hours: 62

For more information on college and university programs visit The American Board of Funeral Service Education at www.abfse.org

Fingerer

A fingerer repairs the damaged outer surface of leather shoes. The fingerer examines shoes for defects, such as scuffs, cracks, and blemishes, spreads glue on the defects and presses the leather with a heated iron rod to seal, buffs the defective area with sandpaper or by holding the shoe against a buffing wheel and wipes the defective area with a rag to remove any foreign material. The fingerer then mixes waxes to obtain a matching color or selects a matching crayon stick and spreads the wax on the defective surface. When finished, the fingerer rubs the repaired area with a rag to polish and blend surfaces.

Find employment in this job by searching your local newspaper 🗞, telephone book ☎, or the Web 💻 under: Leather, Leather Cleaning, Leather Goods-Repair, Leather Goods-Wholesale and Manufacturers, Shoe Repair, Shoe Technicians, Shoes Retail, Shoes-Wholesale and Manufacturers.

Flamer

As an integral part of the shoe industry, a flamer, also known as a homosexual male (not required for the job though) singes excess threads from shoe uppers by using a gas flame or torch or cuts them with a knife or scissors when necessary.

Find employment in this job by searching your local newspaper 📰, telephone book ☎, or the Web 🖥 under: Shoe Repair, Shoe Technicians, Shoes Retail, Shoes-Wholesale and Manufacturers.

Glove Former

Isotoners don't just get that way on their own!

A glove former pulls pairs of gloves (one at a time) over a heated, hand-shaped form and then smoothes the gloves with his or her hands, a cloth, or a brush to shape and press the gloves. The glove former presses the thick portion of heavy gloves by beating the fingertips and seams with a wooden block and then smoothes the gloves between the fingers (also known as the crotch of the glove) by pulling a rake (pronged bar) over the gloved form. Other glove former duties include examining gloves while pressing to detect defects, turning seams inside, and sewing ripped seams and small tears by hand. The glove former may also apply a chemical solution and rub gloves with a cloth to remove stains or apply a chemical or ready-mixed tint with a cloth to restore the original color to the gloves.

Find employment in this job by searching your local newspaper 📰, telephone book ☎, or the Web 🖥 under:

Clothing-Men's-Wholesale and Manufacturers, Clothing-Resale, Clothing-Women's and Misses'-Wholesale and Manufacturers, Gloves.

Gravel Inspector

A gravel inspector makes our roads safer by testing samples of gravel to determine suitability for use in highway construction. The gravel inspector weighs a sample before and after heating to determine its moisture content and screens gravel through numbered screens to determine the coarseness of samples. The gravel inspector also performs other duties in a material testing laboratory, such as hardness tests, breakage tests, density tests for flexible bases, compression and tensile strength tests, and tests for stress and strain durability.

Find employment in this job by searching your local newspaper 🖼, telephone book ☎, or the Web 🖥 under: Asphalt, Construction, Construction Management, Contractors-Driveway, Road Building Contractors, Sand and Gravel, Stone-Building, Stone-Crushed.

Hacker

If you thought of *War Games* or a chronic pflegm-spitter, you're wrong. The most commonly employed hacker lifts green-clay products, such as brick, roofing tile, or quarry flooring tile from a conveyor belt and stacks them in a specified pattern on a kiln car, drier rack, or pallet. Additionally, the hacker may also be responsible for pressing the button that controls the movement of the conveyor belt.

Find employment in this job by searching your local newspaper 📧, telephone book ☎, or the Web 💻 under: Brick-Common and Face, Brick Walkways and Patios, Clay, Floors-Contractors and Builders, Mason Contractors, Roofing Contractors.

Hair Boiler

A hair boiler controls vats that boil animal hair for curling. As a matter of public safety in preventing the transmission of diseases, animal hair products must be boiled. The hair boiler turns the valves needed to admit water and steam into the vats and drains the water from the vats after the hair is boiled.

Animal hair is used for such products as clothing materials, accessories, carpets, hats, paint brushes and piano hammers.

Find employment in this job by searching your local newspaper 📧, telephone book ☎, or the Web 💻 under: Farms, Food Processing, Meat Markets, Meat-Wholesale.

Hay Sorter

A hay sorter removes foreign matter from hay, packs it in a trough, and pushes it toward a machine that bundles and ties it. It may sound unimportant, but the cows sure count on it!

Find employment in this job by searching your local newspaper 📧, telephone book ☎, or the Web 💻 under: Farms, Feed Dealers, Landscape Contractors, Livestock Dealers.

Hooking: Get Paid for Sex and Then Cash in on Your Assets!

Working for an Escort Service
by Marcella Grant

Many women who choose prostitution choose to work for an escort service. If you choose the service wisely and are aware of your own responsibilities, it can provide a positive working experience. Let's go through the process of selecting an agency.

Step one. Shopping for a service. Get all the local publications where sexual services are advertised, and get the yellow pages. If you can, look at old yellow pages as well. What you are checking for is how long a service has been in business. I myself would not work for a service that did not have a listing in the yellow pages under Escorts. There are a lot of fly-by-night services around and they are less likely to really care about either you or their clientele. So check the phone book, and compare it to ads you might see in periodicals. I always avoided services that were blatantly sexual in their ads — it sets up a certain mindset in the client — "I can say or do anything to this girl." Ads that are tasteful send a different message: "I better be nice." So you are looking for longevity, and you are looking to see what kind of image they are giving the client. The other place to check, if you have access to the web, is a site called The World Sex Guide at www.paranoia.com — this site is all posts about sex services from clients or would-be clients, and it's one way to see who is giving good customer service. It's very interesting. Check it out.

Step two. Call the service at a time that many services are closed, morning or early afternoon. They should have a voicemail or machine — anyone who doesn't isn't very professional. What does the outgoing message say? Does it sound like a sleazy phone-sex line? Cross them off your list. The message should be friendly and even flirty, but tasteful. You can leave a message, but be prepared to call back regardless. Many escort services aren't very good about calling women back — it seems to be universal.

Step three. Talking to the service. Be prepared to talk about what sex-work experience you have without actually saying you have had sex for money or that you expect to have sex for money if you work for this service. If you talk openly about sex, they will likely think you are a cop or extremely indiscreet. If they talk openly about sex, rethink working for them. If they will say this to you, they will say it to anyone, and that's how people get busted.

They will ask you what you look like, including your age, weight, height, measurements, hair and eye color. Tell the truth. They are going to see you eventually, and you are just wasting time if you lie. Don't be afraid to sell it a little: "My hair is really silky and I have great legs." But if they aren't looking for new workers, don't try to talk them into it. Note: In my opinion, the best services have phones that are answered by one person and one person only, and that person is a woman. I know women who have worked for services with different phone people, and who have worked for men, but I feel that is a less desirable situation. Multiple phone people make the clients feel less connected than if they have called a number of times and developed a rapport with the phone person. And even the nicest men cannot really understand what it is like to be a woman doing this job. So ask about who answers the phones.

The person on the phone should be pleasant and reasonable. If they are not respectful at this stage, it's not going to get any better. They will ask you if you have a car, and you must have a car; no good agency will drive you, only sleazy ones. You also need a home phone you can be called at, a beeper and preferably a cell phone as well. Most agencies will let you work a little while before asking you to invest in a cell phone if you don't already have one.

They are probably going to want you to commit to working at least three nights a week. I have never figured out why this is so important to most escort services, but it is. There are a lot of flaky and unreliable people in the world and some of them work for escort services, so I assume they are trying to establish some stability and impress upon you that you need to be professional and responsible. It can be worth going along with their rules for a while until you demonstrate your trustworthiness. Once they get to know you, you can frequently get what you want in terms of scheduling, etc.

They may also discuss a deposit. I understand not wanting to be ripped off, but I am not in favor of working for a company that demands you put down a deposit before they will send you on a call. (They are afraid you will take the money and vanish without giving them their cut.) This is something you can decide for yourself, however.

OK, now here is a big thing to watch out for: NEVER work for a service that is willing to send you out on a call sight unseen! This is soooo unprofessional, and anyone who cares so little about their clientele will not care about you either. They should always meet you for an interview. The best services I have worked for met me in a restaurant or a nice quiet bar. Dress like you would on a call. (More on that in a minute.) At this point, there may be some more open talk about sex, but let them initiate it. They should tell you what their hours are, what areas they service, what the rates are and what the fee split is. They may also tell you about how many girls they have, and beware of services that have more than eight; one person cannot keep track of eight people at a time, which means you won't get as many calls or they don't keep good tabs on where you are, which is bad. If you don't like the person, don't work for them. You will have to trust the person answering the phone or else you will not be comfortable going on the calls. You should feel that the person is concerned about your safety and security.

So, let's assume that everything is good, you have found a service you like, and it's your first night on call. Be ready when you said you would; you don't have to sit around in full drag, but be able to leave the house in 20 minutes or less. When the phone rings, you should be given the following info: the client's full name, if he has used the service before, and where he is. (If it is a private home, you may be given his phone number to call and get directions.) As a new worker, you should not be sent to a new client on your first call; more likely the phone person will send you to a regular client who will call back to the service after you leave to give you a review. Some services want you to call the client to say hi, and tell them you are on your way. Some don't. It varies.

What to wear: Well, as outrageously as I may dress in my personal life, I think it's best to be understated on the job. Think of it in terms of cues. He already knows you are a prostitute when you arrive, so that is cueing his behavior. Balancing the "bad girl" image with a "nice girl" message of the subtle dress or suit makes him more likely to treat you like a lady, which is what you want. So think expensive looking, classy, subtly sexy dresses, and skirts. I tend not to wear pants unless I know the client well and know he is OK with that. Underneath, I wear pretty, matched lingerie, particularly with garter belts or thigh-hi stockings. Clients love that.

You should be told to call into the service when you arrive, and they should ask you if everything is OK. The service should also call you when it is time to leave unless you call first to say you are leaving. If it is a new client, you may be told to check his ID, and to ask to see a plane ticket, etc., to "make sure" he is not a cop. There is a lot of gossip and conventional wisdom about how to tell if someone is a cop, and the fact is there is no absolutely foolproof way. Be very wary of someone who says, "So, you are gonna have sex with me if I give you this money, right?" Questions like those are red flags — I have had real clients say things like that to me, but be careful of anyone who questions you in such blunt terms. You can give a vague answer "Oh darlin', we are going to get along just fine, don't you worry!" But be careful and always trust your instincts. I have never been arrested, and I believe it is because I chose my services carefully and always listened to my feelings about the clients. One of my tricks is to not take the money up front if I don't know the guy. Yes, you stand a slight chance of getting stiffed, but it would be much harder to make a case against you if you did not ask for or accept money. I have never been stiffed for the fee, and frankly, I do better with tips when I get paid afterwards.

Speaking of pay, rates vary from city to city. Here in Seattle it's running from around 150 dollars per hour to 180. Be prepared to pay the service 60 or 70 dollars of that. You will get tipped sometimes, other times you won't. No good agency should take any part of any tip you get. The average on the number of calls per night is from one to three, depending on how busy it is. There will be nights when you don't get any. If you don't get a call three nights in a row, talk to the service. Is it unusually slow? Is there anything wrong with your job performance? Don't be angry or abusive, though — if the phone isn't ringing much on a particular night, there is nothing the service can do to make them.

One book you might read to give you more information about escort services is called *Mayflower Madame* by a woman called Sydney Biddle Barrows. She ran a service in New York and this is her tell-all book. I think she has prettied up things a bit in her book, but it has a lot of good tips for escorts. I see it in both new and used bookstores all the time.

Working for a good service that treats you well and has a good clientele is one of the best ways I know of to be a prostitute. Just remember, never do anything that makes you feel bad. It's up to you to know your limits and maintain your emotional and physical boundaries. Take care of yourself first and foremost. You can always make more money another night. Sex work can be draining. It's important to nurture yourself.

Verbal Marketing Techniques From a Sex Worker Named Chavi

If you're a sex worker looking to change to a career in the straight working world, you're ahead of the game. Below you'll find out how to assess the skills you currently have and how to apply them to a "regular" job. Remember, sex workers and baseball players usually retire early — and we can both guess who ESPN isn't going to offer a job to!

Some of the most amazing artists, sales people, personal trainers, therapists and body-workers I've met are or have been sex workers. There is a natural entrepreneurial climate that prevails throughout the industry. For instance, I know this ex-peepshow gal who can sell anything to anyone. She is now a hotshot ladder climber at a computer company. While working in the booth she honed her "verbal marketing technique" as she hustled $20 from some guy who wanted to glance at her twat. She later was able to harness the technique and use it to get anything she wanted. The moral of the story is you should always keep the "verbal marketing technique" in mind when feeling discouraged about your career options.

Using the skills you have learned as a sex worker:
1. *Make-up and presentation.* You know when you look good for a customer. You know you make more money when

you look good. The same applies in the straight world. A self-confident and well-presented person is going to leave an impression on any employer.

2. *Saying the right things at the right time.* More often than not you know when and what to say to your client. The words might be different during an interview but it's still the same technique.

3. *Education.* So they say you can give a good blowjob. Blowjobs take time to learn. The same goes for many professions in the world.

4. *Marketing.* You can sell your sexy persona to any client. Why not sell a modified version of that persona to employers, art buyers, potential product buyers, clients, etc.

5. *Passion.* A passion you have should always be pursued.

6. *Customer service.* You know what they want and you know what to give them.

Houseboy

A houseboy is typically a homosexual male employed to perform light housekeeping duties as well as sexual favors when requested. A houseboy is usually paid well, with tips on top of his base salary, and gifts and bonuses are commonplace. A houseboy can be employed by either a male or female and doesn't object to sexual favors with a female, as the females are usually extremely wealthy, and the fringe benefits (such as flex-time, drinks and lounging poolside) are great.

Find employment in this job by searching your local newspaper 📰, telephone book ☎, or the Web 💻 under: Building Cleaning-Interior, Escort Services, House Cleaning, Janitor Service.

Impregnating Helper

An impregnating helper assists in the impregnating of electrical products, such as capacitors and coils — not women! An impregnating helper performs the following duties: loads capacitors into ovens by using a hoist, and connects the filler pipe of each capacitor to the pipes of a vacuum system and turns valves to start and stop the vacuum and regulates the control equipment during the impregnation process while under the supervision of the impregnator. Other duties of the impregnating helper include reading vacuum gauges and the capacitance bridge to determine their degrees and recording and reporting the readings to the impregnator.

Find employment in this job by searching your local newspaper 📰, telephone book ☎, or the Web 💻 under: Electric Contractors, Electric Equipment-Repair and Service, Electric Instruments, Electric Motors-Repairs.

Irish-Moss Gatherer

Commercially, Irish moss is used as a stabilizing agent and thickener in chocolate milk, ice cream, baked goods, and many other food items. It is also incorporated as an emulsifier into cosmetics and skin lotions because it is a moist soothing emollient.

An Irish-moss gatherer gathers Irish moss from rocks by hand or by using a rake, and hauls it into a boat, then transfers the moss to land where it is washed and bleached by an Irish-moss bleacher.

Find employment in this job by searching your local newspaper 📰, telephone book ☎, or the Web 💻 under: Consumer Goods-Manufacturing, Food Processing, Food Products.

Ladle Pourer

A ladle pourer casts refined lead into molds as the molds move along a conveyor belt. The ladle pourer also connects pipelines from a kettle to a ladle and preheats pipes, valves, and the ladle with a gas burner to prevent hardening of the metal. The ladle pourer controls the flow of metal into the ladle, pours lead into molds by tilting the ladle, and skims oxide from the surface of metal in molds. Makes you wonder what a ladle pourer can do with simple soup!

Find employment in this job by searching your local newspaper 📰, telephone book ☎, or the Web 💻 under: Metal Distributors, Metal Fabricators, Metal Goods-Manufacturers, Metal Products, Metal Products-Manufacturing, Metal Specialties, Metalizing.

Load Dispatcher

A load dispatcher coordinates the activities of personnel engaged in operating generating stations, substations, and the lines of electric power systems or electrified railway systems to ensure the adequate production and distribution of electricity to meet power demands.

In smaller systems, the load dispatcher calculates load estimates according to corrected weather and consumer-demand records and notifies the switchboard operator at generating stations of the electric power required to meet fluctuating demands.

In larger systems, the load dispatcher receives load schedules for various generating stations from their power plant operators. The load dispatcher also monitors the control board that shows the operating condition of lines and equipment throughout the system and makes adjustments or directs workers to make adjustments as conditions warrant.

The load dispatcher directs substation operators and other workers to deenergize malfunctioning circuits or adjusts switches to ensure the safety of maintenance crews and avoid interruptions of service during repairs. The load dispatcher notifies maintenance crews of the location and deenergization of troubled sectors, and verifies that workers are clear of repaired equipment before directing energization of circuits, contacts other utilities by telephone to arrange exchange of power according to existing contracts or in an emergency and coordinates tie-ins with other systems and compiles operational records. The load dispatcher also operates a computer console, which is programmed to automatically perform load-control functions, calculates the discharge rate of water in reservoirs utilizing reports of rain, river flow, and water level in reservoirs, and directs setting of watergates at hydroelectric plants to coordinate water flow and power generation with irrigation and flood control requirements and may compute bills for power delivered to interconnected utilities.

Find employment in this job by searching your local newspaper 🗞, telephone book ☎, or the Web 🖥 under: Electric Companies, Electric Contractors, Electronic Testing

Equipment, Electronics-Research and Development, Power Protection, Power Supply Systems, Power Transmission.

Lozenge Maker Helper

A lozenge maker helper operates a machine that rolls dough into sheets, and then embosses and cuts the dough into candy lozenges. The lozenge maker helper helps to position and secure cutting and embossing dies in place by using a wrench, adjusts the ram stroke of the cutting die to synchronize it with the speed of the dough rollers and discharge conveyor, turns the handwheel to adjust clearance between rollers, and dumps lozenge dough into the hopper and starts the machine. The lozenge maker helper also sprinkles cornstarch onto dough to prevent sticking to rollers and dies. The lozenge maker helper examines and weighs formed lozenges for conformity to size, shape, and weight specifications, readjusts roller speed and clearance to meet product standards, and may adjust printer bars on machines to print or emboss designs on lozenges before cutting.

Find employment in this job by searching your local newspaper 📰, telephone book ☎, or the Web 💻 under: Candy-Retail, Candy-Wholesale and Manufacturers, Food Processing, Food Products, Foods-Ready to Serve.

Lusterer

A lusterer isn't pining away somewhere for someone he or she can't have — a lusterer is too busy applying paint to the exterior or interior of glassware such as tumblers, vases, or bowls to tint glass and to apply luster. The lusterer mixes color with oil and water to obtain the desired consistency, centers glassware on a balanced wheel and balances glassware on the wheel with weights, and turns a pivot pole with one hand to rotate the wheel and glassware, and holds a paint brush to the glassware while resting an arm on a support to steady the hand to apply a thin layer of paint. The lusterer also examines glassware for brush strokes and places painted glassware onto a moving conveyor.

Find employment in this job by searching your local newspaper 📰, telephone book ☎, or the Web 🖥 under: Glass Coating and Tinting, Glass-Ornamental, Glaziers.

Mangler

A mangler tends a mangle (what else?) that wets-out cloth or applies finishing chemicals, such as size starch, synthetic resins, or cellulose derivatives to cloth. The mangler positions trucks of cloth at the feed-end of the machine and threads cloth through guides, under an immersion roll, and through an expander attachment and squeeze rolls, or sews the end of the cloth to the leader in the machine, using a portable sewing machine. The mangler also turns a valve to admit water, starch, or finishing solution to the trough of the mangle, turns the handwheel to set the pressure of the squeeze rollers according to the thickness of the cloth. Observes the flow of the cloth through the mangle to detect holes and torn selvages, cuts flaws from the cloth by using scissors, and sews the ends of the cloth together.

i—Find employment in this job by searching your local newspaper 📰, telephone book ☎, or the Web 💻 under: Cloth Cutting, Clothing-Men's-Wholesale and Manufacturers, Clothing-Women's and Misses'-Wholesale and Manufacturers, Fabric Treatment, Fabrics-Wholesale and Manufacturers.

Mud Boss

A mud boss drains, filters, dries, crushes, and packages slime from electrolytic tanks, preparatory to the recovery of valuable metals, such as gold, silver, platinum, and vanadium. To do all this, the mud boss pulls a lever to drain and filter slime from electrolytic tanks into a storage tank, then drains the slime into a machine to subject it to heat and pressure to remove moisture. Next, the mud boss starts a conveyor to transport dry slime to an automatic grinder machine, observes the flow of the slime from the grinder into the container, weighs the container, and marks the weight on the container and tally sheet, inspects tanks for leaks and other defects and collects samples of liquids for analysis. The mud boss may also tend a machine which dries and presses slime into cakes for shipment, transfer electrolyte from one tank to another by passing it through an intermediate steam-heated tank, offsetting evaporation by adding hot water, or may smooth the surface of starting sheets with sandpaper to remove pits and scratches.

i—Find employment in this job by searching your local newspaper 📰, telephone book ☎, or the Web 💻 under: Contractors-Excavating, Drilling Contractors, Metal Specialties,

Smelters and Refiners-Precious Metals, Tank-Testing and Inspection, Tank and Trap Cleaning.

Necker

A necker feeds rolls of cardboard and fabric into a machine that automatically wraps materials around each other to form cardboard necks (filler between the case and lining of a jewelry box). The necker is also responsible for setting controls to cut strips to a prescribed length, observing the machine to detect malfunctions, and dumping the strips into a basket for further processing.

Find employment in this job by searching your local newspaper 📧, telephone book ☎, or the Web 💻 under: Box Manufacturers, Equipment and Supplies, Jewelers-Manufacturers, Jewelers-Retail, Jewelers-Supplies and Findings, Jewelers-Wholesale.

Nibbler

A nibbler cuts metal plates, sheets, or structural shapes into specified radial or irregular shapes by the action of reciprocating cutting knives or punches. The nibbler positions and clamps a specified cutter or punch into the ram and bed of the machine, turns thumbscrews to adjust the depth of the stroke to the thickness of metal, turns a handwheel to set a specified distance between the cutter or punch and the center point of the turntable or fixtures, using a built-in scale or rule, clamps guide and drive rollers over the work piece, depresses a pedal which activates the ram and feed rollers to cut or punch along the radius and guides the work piece manually along the cutting lines or template to cut irregular shapes. Other duties of the nibbler include laying out guidelines onto the work piece by tracing from the template, matting a drill center hole into the work piece, using a portable drill and beveling edges of steel plates, using a portable pneumatic nibbler.

Find employment in this job by searching your local newspaper 📰, telephone book ☎, or the Web 💻 under: Metal Fabricators, Metal Goods-Manufacturers, Metal Products, Metal Products-Manufacturers, Metal Sawing and Cut Off Services, Metal Specialties.

Nut Grinder

A nut grinder grinds nutmeats into meal. The nut grinder turns a thumbscrew or handwheel to adjust the distance between the grinding rollers, fills the machine hopper with almond meats, and starts the machine and places a container at the discharge end of the machine to catch the emerging nut meal. The nut grinder also inspects samples of ground nut meal for fineness of grind, and adjusts rollers when necessary to ensure that nut meats are ground to specification and may start a vacuum hose to remove foreign matter from nut meats.

Find employment in this job by searching your local newspaper 📰, telephone book ☎, or the Web 💻 under: Farms, Food Processing, Food Products, Nuts-Edible-Retail.

Odd Shoe Examiner

An odd shoe examiner examines shoe uppers for defective leather parts and distributes replacement parts to a processing area, but the job doesn't stop there. The odd shoe examiner also cuts the stitching in shoe uppers with a knife or scissors and rips out defective parts, writes specifications for replacement parts on a work order and delivers it to the initial processing area and, acting as liaison with other departments, the odd shoe examiner then carries replacement parts to and from various departments to accomplish the specified processing, such as cutting, marking, and stitching, delivers replacement parts to the fitting department for assembly to the uppers of shoes and converses with department supervisors to correct irregular flow of replacement parts.

Find employment in this job by searching your local newspaper 📰, telephone book ☎, or the Web 🖥 under: Shoe Repair, Shoe Technicians, Shoes Retail, Shoes-Wholesale and Manufacturers.

Heidi Fleiss: Pandering Potentials

Heidi Fleiss, dubbed "The Hollywood Madam" by the press, was arrested in 1993 for tax evasion, money laundering, and conspiracy related to the high-priced call-girl ring she operated. Her notorious "Black Book" of clients is said to have included the names of many prominent Hollywood individuals, among them Charlie Sheen, who reportedly paid more than $50,000 for about thirty "dates." Heidi Fleiss was also rumored to be on the payrolls of the biggest studios in Hollywood.

America watched during her high-profile "Court TV" trial as Heidi Fleiss entered the courtroom vamped-out and wearing dark shades. She laughed and mocked the jury and her accusers as prosecutors called them to testify on the stand. During the time of the trial, the always-enterprising Heidi started her own clothing line called "Heidi Wear" and worked the talk show circuit.

With headquarters being Michael Douglas' former home, at the ripe old age of 27, Heidi was taking 40% off the average $1500 per night fee her girls received. Heidi's clients were the "cream of the crop" (pardon the expression): A-list actors, musicians and moguls. She once put it in perspective like this: "I knew all the richest men. I had all the connections. I was the best there will ever be!"

Currently, Heidi is still a success. She was released from prison in 1998, saved a man from committing suicide, began dating movie star Tom Sizemore, penned a book on her exploits called *Pandering* and recently released the notorious DVD *Sex Tips With Heidi Fleiss*. With all this going on, Heidi Fleiss still manages to maintain her Heidi Wear business.

How does one get to this happy place? Money and good-looking friends. Get your best girlfriends together and start today: Go to parties and political events and you're a shoo-in! Madams differ from pimps in that they are kind, nurturing, and treat their ladies well. Good luck!

Phone Sex Operator:
Get Paid to Talk Dirty

Phone sex is a multi-billion-dollar business. Even during these times of emerging computer technology, with chat rooms and cybersex, phone sex jobs are on the rise and have even begun to be recognized as legitimate employment. A phone sex operator in Florida was recently awarded disability payments by the state for injuries she sustained on the job (wrist and muscle problems from masturbating so much to please her customers on the other end of the line!).

Phone sex jobs offer flexible hours and wardrobes (you don't even need to dress or leave your house!), competitive pay and health benefits. Your local newspaper should have listings for phone sex opportunities or check out the resources listed below.

Telephone Fantasy Operators
San Diego, CA
619-260-6905
Full-time positions available

Telephone Chatters for Adult Service
Nationwide
800-315-9069
Full-time and Part-time starting at $8.50/hour

Telephone Actors and Actresses
Los Angeles
213-962-0790
Pay starts at $15/will train

Party Line Operators
Woodland Hills, CA
818-594-3941
All shifts available

Telephone Chatters
Los Angeles
818-558-7522
Work from home/bonus included

Pile-Driver

"Hi-Yah!!!"

A pile-driver operates (of course) a pile-driver mounted on skids, barge, crawler treads, or a locomotive crane to drive piling as foundations for structures, such as buildings, bridges, and piers. The pile-driver moves hand and foot levers to control diesel, electric, gasoline, or steam-powered hoisting equipment to position piling leads, hoist piling into leads, and position the hammer over the top of the pile. The pile-driver moves the levers and turns the valves to activate a power-driven hammer, or raise and lower a drophammer, which drives piles to the required depth. A pile-driver's title may differ according to the type of power used to activate the pile-driver: compressed-air-pile-driver operator; diesel-pile-driver operator; or by the type of piles driven: concrete-pile-driver operator; sheet-pile-driver operator; wood-pile-driver operator; or by the type of mounting used: pile-driver operator, barge mounted. Other titles, which may be designated include: drop-hammer-pile-driver operator; electric-pile-driver operator; steam-pile-driver operator.

Find employment in this job by searching your local newspaper 🗞, telephone book ☎, or the Web 💻 under: Contractors-Building, Contractors-General, Contractors-Marine, Crane Service.

Pillowcase Turner

A pillowcase turner tends a machine that turns pillowcases right-side-out and stretches the material to remove wrinkles. The pillowcase turner turns dials to adjust turner arms according to the width of the pillowcases and to adjust the speed and throw of the discharge mechanism. The pillow turner then positions a pillowcase on the arms and depresses a pedal to activate the mechanism that inverts the pillowcase and discharges the article onto a rack and may turn pillowcases by hand or using a turning stand.

i Find employment in this job by searching your local newspaper 📰, telephone book ☎, or the Web 💻 under: Bedding, Beds, Fabric Treatment, Fabrics-Wholesale and Manufacturers

Pimpin'
(not to be confused with Mackin') 101

Overview of the Pimp Game

In all businesses you have the employers and the employees. You have drones, worker bees and a queen bee. You have the owner of a basketball team; you have basketball players. You have a coach and you have fans.

The owner (like the pimp) is usually quiet, stays in the background, is mysterious and, of course, powerful. He is seldom seen and almost never seen with his players. He keeps his distance from all aspects of the game that don't directly concern him. He's there for the draft and after that the player deals with the coach and agents and other players. The owner most likely has never been a basketball player. The owner puts in the least amount of effort and reaps the highest reward, from the labor of others.

Loyal fans mean cash for the owner, but a player's time is limited. A good owner and a well-schooled player both sell as much as they can while they can. They both know that with every ho there comes a time when the tricks (fans in basketball, johns in pimping) stop biting.

If the owner is the pimp and the players are hos, then who is the coach? The coach is your bottom woman. The bottom woman is the first ho you knock (break down into total submission) and the most dedicated. Once you knock the bottom woman, she will go out and recruit hos for you. Just like a coach, the bottom woman knows everything about the game and is usually a former player. The bottom woman is usually the least paid, works the hardest, and deals with the hos on a daily basis.

The Pimp Defined

To become a pimp you need to commit social suicide. Withdraw from family, friends, and places you are known to frequent. You must appear too busy for day-to-day socializing. Example: if you see certain people twice a week, drop it to twice a month. Do more listening than talking and never be asked to leave. Leave in the middle of a conversation, preferably at its height. That will show that you have no interest. When you speak, you will have your follower's undivided attention. Your money, time and attention all must be spent on you. You are the only thing that consumes your attention. If it's not about you, you don't care! Your life and activities must remain a mystery. It's the mystery that draws your followers closer to the flame. Nothing excites you. Nothing angers you; it's all beneath you. You make yourself special. When an attractive woman walks by, you yawn.

You also need to master the art of being felt without being seen or heard. When you walk into a room, pause, look all around the room, then enter. The words, "I don't know," can't ever come out of your mouth. If you don't know something, then the proper response for the pimp is, "I don't care."

A ho to a pimp is worth nothing. She is actually worth everything, but you must make her believe she is worthless. A pimp buys the souls of hos. Remember, your power is your anonymity, and your arrogance and distance are your protection.

How to Knock Your Ho and Start the Dough Flowing

You take a girl from her world into another. You take her on a tour first and show her how she can be #1. Then, drop her back into her world. She will begin to compare your fantasy to her reality and begin to rebel. In the beginning, whenever she gets upset or in a jam, she'll call you and you must help her. This is the first step to getting her to totally depend on you. You'll start to dress her, think for her, own her. If you are sexually active with her, then slow it down to no more than once a week. After sex, take her shopping. She will then develop a sense of accomplishment. The shopping, after a month, will be replaced by cash. The lovemaking turns to raw sex. She'll start to crave intimacy and begin to do whatever it takes to get back in your good graces. You have broken her spirit and she has no self-value. Now, put a price tag on what you've manufactured.

You need to pick a girl with little or no self-esteem who wants something, be it fame, love, money, respect, security or whatever. That whatever is something she is willing to sacrifice all to have. That is the thing you as the pimp need to attain before she does. You then sell it to her for her soul. You are the cause as well as the solution to all her problems. You give her the poison and then sell her the cure.

You don't do anything for her without receiving sex. You have to get it in her head that money and favors come from sex. After your victim is in the habit of exchanging sex for favors, then it's time to test her. Her first trick should be with someone she's met, perhaps a friend of yours. If she passes the test, you're in business. The average pimp commission ranges from 60-100%.

That's it in a nutshell. Your bottom woman is ready to go recruit your entourage and after a few tricks, you'll be counting the cash. Pimping is easier than you think — as long as you don't steal another pimp's ho.

So What's a Mack Then?

A mack practices a style of pimping that is almost opposite to the reclusive lifestyle of a pimp. A mack works out front, in the open. He is highly visible. He is liked and admired up close. Charm is his main weapon. The biggest difference between a pimp and a mack is that the mack enjoys the fruit of his labors.

A mack mingles among commoners to build his power. A mack is cunning, cold, and a con to the core. The mack is extremely dangerous because he's full of smiles, firm handshakes and inviting eye contact. Like a snake, he appears to be your friend. He sells his ho with the idea of team or family. A ho feels like she's making an investment with a mack, as opposed to the complete servitude relationship with a pimp.

A mack has all the skills and desires of a pimp, but what separates the mack is that the mack's desire for money and approval outweighs his lust for power. A mack enjoys life, women, and everything he can consume for self-gratification. Macks set limits, as opposed to pimps, who will sink to unfathomed lows.

For more information visit www.thepimpgame.com

Breaking Into **Porn**

America is the world's leading producer of porn, and that means JOBS! The L.A. County Economic Development Corporation estimates the number of jobs created by the porn industry is between 10,000 and 20,000.

The porn industry releases approximately 10,000 titles a year. In comparison, Hollywood only churns out about 400 theatrical releases a year (ironically cashing in on the porn industry, i.e., *Boogie Nights, The People vs. Larry Flynt,* etc.). The porn industry pulls in an average of $10 billion a year from video, cable, DVD, the Internet and phone sex.

Is Porn For You?

People get into porn for many reasons.

Some do it for the *money.* Porn offers a variety of work situations: full-time, part-time, flex-time and good pay! If you get into porn and save your money, invest wisely and live moderately, you can get by working just a couple of days a week!

Some do it for the *fame.* Fame is undoubtedly a tantalizing prospect for anyone who dances naked in front of their bedroom mirror to the applause of an imaginary audience. With fame you also meet famous people. Most porn stars date rock stars. At the top of her game, porn starlet Savannah dated Pauly Shore, Vince Neil, Billy Idol, Slash and Marky Mark.

Some do it for *attention.* Like a sales job, you either have a born knack for it or you don't!

Some do it for the *sex.* A lot of Americans just can't get enough sex, so what's better than getting paid to have sex all day?

Some do it to *break into acting.* True, some porn stars have gone onto achieve great success in legitimate films. Traci Lords went from underage porn star to starring in movies such as *Cry Baby*, to recording her own techno album and most recently appearing as a series regular on the Sci-Fi channel.

So how can you tell if you'll really be able to go through with it? Here's a test. First ask yourself, "Am I OK with what I'm doing?" If your answer is yes, the next test will prove it. Gather 10 friends, get naked in front of them, and masturbate to orgasm. If you can handle that, you're ready for porn.

The Stigma

Porn continues to be the most convenient scapegoat (next to homosexuality) for every social ill from AIDS to the Mafia to bad breath. Porn stars, porn sets, porn producers, porn directors, porn distributors, porn retailers (and even porn fans) have all been busted countless times over the years.

Much of the misunderstanding of today's porn industry is connected to the social stigmas of the past. Obscenity laws in the 70s were poorly defined and there were many instances of women being forced into sexual acts and exploitation. Porn makers frequently made films that depicted incest, violent rape fantasies and bestiality (sex with animals).

Nowadays the depiction of any violent, non-consensual sex, urination or defecation, and child pornography is illegal and strictly enforced. Because 90% of all porn is generated in Los Angeles, there are approximately 8,000 full-time cops constantly monitoring the situation.

A Day In the Life

Usually the porn shoot starts with a few snap shots for the cover of the video box. Next, the dialog scenes (nothing different from any other film set here.) THEN — the real business begins.

Many times two films are shot at once: a hardcore and a softcore. Hardcore is "balls out" (as they call it in the biz) with everything shown. The softcore version gets recut with no shots of penetration, erect penises, or bodily fluids. Softcore versions are usually sold to cable and pay-per-view channels.

There are a requisite number of positions and combinations that can be scheduled by the director. These include fellatio, cunniligus, missionary-style, doggie-style, cowgirl, reverse cowgirl, double-penetration, double-pussy penetration and double-anal penetration — ouch!!! There are six basic sexual-partner combinations: solo masturbation, girl-girl, boy-girl, girl-girl-boy, boy-boy-girl, boy-boy and the notorious orgy.

A porn shoot can last anywhere from one day to five days, depending on the budget. The director is usually no more than 15 feet away from the performers' genitals at any given time. The crew can range from one cameraman to 20 or 30 people. High-end porn locations might be classy studios with multiple sets and air conditioning, while low-end sets might be in someone's basement.

The Business of Porn

Although cities like New York and San Francisco contribute plenty of porn, to make it, you need to move to LA. Not only are 50 of the 85 porn companies based there, it's also home to the largest congregation of porn stars: 1,600 and counting!

The heart of the porn business is the San Fernando Valley of Los Angeles, often referred to as "Silicone Valley" or the "Valley of Sin." Some of the hottest adult spots in the valley include Sherman Oaks, Canoga Park, Van Nuys, Studio City and Chatsworth.

Money

The highest paid female performers work under contract and can earn between $80,000 and $100,000 a year for appearing in about 20 sex scenes and making around a dozen personal appearances. Freelance female performers working without a contract can expect to earn as much as $5,000 to $7,000 a day. A typical pay breakdown works like this:

Fellatio = $300-$350

Lesbian Scene = $400-$600

Boy-Girl Scene = $500-$700

Double Penetration = $800-$2,000

Anal, Double Anal or Double Pussy = $1,000 and up

Male performers on the average make less than females. The average daily rate for a male performer is $150-$600 per day and includes two pop shots. (Pop shots, also known as "money shots" or "cum shots," are when a man ejaculates on camera.) Still shoots can earn you from $50 to $200. Typically, male performers go by the day rate or negotiate their rate based on the number of pop shots they will be required to provide.

Agents and Other Resources

Just like mainstream Hollywood, agents are your ticket in. They get you the gigs, fight to get you a good going rate and have all the connections. Below is a partial list of some of the top porn agencies. If they don't take you on as a client they can usually give you advice on bettering your chances for breaking into the business.

World Modeling Talent Agency
4523 Van Nuys Boulevard, Suite 203
Sherman Oaks, CA 91403
Phone: 818-986-4316
Fax: 818-986-9487
Internet: www.worldmodeling.com

Reb's Pretty Girl International
7494 Santa Monica Boulevard, 2nd Floor
West Hollywood, CA 90048
Phone: 323-882-8262
Internet: www.prettygirl.com

Beautiful Models International
11385 Expo Boulevard, Suite 150
Los Angeles, CA 90064
Phone: 310-207-4622
Internet: www.better-business.com/bmifmod.htm

CHN International
7428 Santa Monica Boulevard
Los Angeles, CA 90046
Phone: 323-874-8252

Some other useful resources include:

Fans of X-Rated Entertainment (F.O.X.E.)
8231 DeLongpre Avenue, Suite 1
West Hollywood, CA 90046
Phone: 323-650-7121

Adultex (Adult Entertainment Expo)
Phone: 765-651-9872
Internet: www.adultex.com

AVN Award Show (the largest adult awards show)
Phone: 800-521-2474
Internet: www.avn.com/awards/menu.html

Adult Industry Medical Healthcare Foundation (AIM)
14241 Ventura Boulevard, Suite 105
Sherman Oaks, CA 91423
Phone: 818-981-5681

North Hollywood 10-Minute HIV Test Center
12910 Victory Boulevard
North Hollywood, CA 91601
Phone: 818-760-4500

Adult Stars Magazine
Phone: 954-458-0021
Internet: www.adultstarsmagazine.com

Fantasy Outlet (DVD's, videos and more)
584 Castro, #134
San Francisco, CA 94114
Phone: 415-376-3504
Internet: www.fantasyoutlet.com

Retail Slut (clothing and accessories)
7308 Melrose Avenue
Phone: 323-934-1339

Le Sex Shoppe (porn toys and accessories)
6315½ Hollywood Boulevard
Phone: 323-464-9435

Pulverizer

Type 1: This pulverizer grinds dried flake albumen into granules. This pulverizer starts the grinder mill and opens the chute gate on the machine hopper to direct flake albumen between grinder rolls. Using a scoop, the pulverizer fills the hopper with flake albumen, and then examines granules and adjusts machine roller settings as required, using handtools, to ensure the albumen is ground to the specified size.

Type 2: This pulverizer pulverizes lumps of salicylic acid. This pulverizer starts the machine and flow of lumps of salicylic acid into the machine, dumps pulverized salicylic acid into drums and weighs and seals the drums and uses a powered handtruck to transport or stack the filled drums.

Type 3: This pulverizer pulverizes pieces of enamel to be used in decorating jewelry settings, using mortar and pestle. This pulverizer places lumps of enamel crystals in a mortar and crushes them by striking the pestle with a hammer, pours pulverized material through a sieve and recrushes those pieces that do not pass through the sieve.

Find employment in this job by searching your local newspaper 📰, telephone book ☎, or the Web 💻 under: Contractors-Building, Contractors-General, Contractors-Marine, Crane Service.

Quick Sketch Artist

The quick sketch artist (as opposed to the slow sketch artist!) sketches the likenesses of customers. The quick sketch artist poses subjects to accentuate their most pleasing features and draws a likeness, using pencil, charcoal, pastels, or other medium. The quick sketch artist may draw sketches from photographs or draw exaggerated likenesses and be designated a caricaturist. The quick sketch artist can be found in busy public areas, amusement parks, or at a police station drawing sketches of criminals based on eyewitness descriptions.

Find employment in this job by searching your local newspaper 🖼️, telephone book ☎, or the Web 💻 under: Artists-Fine Arts. Check also the blue pages under Law Enforcement.

Reamer

A reamer is a title generally reserved for your mother when she bitches you out (it doesn't matter how old you are), but in the working world there are two specific classifications.

Type 1: This reamer reams the center holes of balance wheels subsequent to a recessing operation to clean the holes, using a hand reamer and loupe.

Type 2: This reamer reams drilled holes in metal work pieces, using handtools. The reamer inserts a reamer (straight-fluted rotary cutting tool) into the hole and twists and pushes it to enlarge, smooth, or improve the roundness of the hole, before verifying hole specifications, using a plug gauge. The Reamer may also place work pieces in a vise when reaming out the hole.

Find employment in this job by searching your local newspaper 🖼️, telephone book ☎, or the Web 💻 under: Metal Goods-Manufacturers, Metal Products, Metal Products-Manufacturers, Metal Sawing and Cut Off Services, Tool Grinding Industrial, Tools-Hand-Manufacturers, Tools-Manufacturers.

Making Money as a
Research Study Subject

Surely you've seen the ads in your newspaper's classified section: "Are You a Pregnant Teen?" "Have You Been Diagnosed with Irritable Bowel Syndrome?" "Feeling Sad or Depressed or Not Yourself?" Basically if you fit the headline requirement, that's all there is to it. If you live near a college, university, or large pharmaceutical company you have the best opportunity to participate in a research study. I live in Connecticut, not far from Yale, and when money gets tight, I donate myself. You don't even have to have a problem to participate, although there seems to be an abundance of drug abuse and mental health studies.

Most recently I participated in a bone-density study. In addition to the $500 dollars (pay varies depending on the study) I received for participating in the study, I also received free meals three times a day for two weeks (the duration of the study). The meals were a way for the doctors to ensure I was eating a balanced diet while they performed weekly blood drawings and urinalyses. So there you have it — cold cash and hot meals — and all you have to do is be you! Some studies require you remain onsite — so there you have it again — housing too! Here are some of the kinds of ads you're likely to see:

***

HEALTHY VOLUNTEERS BETWEEN THE AGES OF 21-30
Are needed for studies at Yale/VA Alcohol Research Center.
If eligible, subjects are paid $100 per test day.

***

WOULD YOU LIKE TO STOP DRINKING?
Free 30 day Inpatient Alcohol Treatment is available for participants in return for research participation involving brain-imaging scans. You may be eligible if you are 30 to 55 years old, medically healthy and currently abusing alcohol. Several studies are now being conducted. In addition to free treatment, you can earn from $300 to $1,150 for your full participation.

***

PICTURE YOUR BRAIN
Healthy Children and Adults, between the ages of 12 and 45, for a Yale study of brain structure and function using magnetic resonance imaging (MRI) and brain EEG. You will be asked to provide information about your medical and psychiatric history, alcohol and drug use and will be given more information about the tests involved. Tests will be scheduled at your convenience. You will be paid for your participation.

***

DO YOU USE COCAINE?
If so, you may qualify for a Yale inpatient research study seeking treatment and non-treatment cocaine users. You will be paid for your participation.

***

These ads appeared in the *New Haven Advocate* newspaper, April 25, 2002. Check your local listings. Note that you must be 18 years of age to participate in most studies.

Ripper

The most famous ripper, of course, being Jack, one would be hard pressed to find steady employment like that now-a-days, although you might land an appearance on *Dateline*, which could be good for your career.

Type 1: This ripper uses a flaring machine to assemble display stands consisting of a tube with disks attached to either end. The ripper starts by inserting the ends of the tube through a hole in the disk, setting the tube in a jig on a machine table, and starting the machine. The ripper then depresses a pedal to raise the table and force the upper end of the tube against the rotating flaring tool to hold the disk on the tube and may glue felt over the outside faces of the disks.

Type 2: This ripper, using a razor blade, scissors, or seam ripper, rips stitches from sections of articles or garments to prepare them for resewing. The ripper pulls out loose threads and may be designated a garment ripper for alterations.

Find employment in this job by searching your local newspaper ▦, telephone book ☎, or the Web ▭ under: Cloth Cutting, Clothing-Men's-Wholesale and Manufacturers, Clothing-Women's and Misses'-Wholesale and Manufacturers, Display Designers and Producers, Display Fixtures and Materials, Display Installation Services, Seamstresses, Sewing Contractors.

Rod Puller

A rod puller operates a coiling device that coils hot rod, wire, or tubing from an extrusion press or rolling mill. The rod puller adjusts the coiler reel according to a specified size and coil, using handtools, inserts the end of the rod, tube, or wire in an automatic coiling rack and moves controls to start the coiler, guides straight lengths of the rod or tube along the table to avoid stretching or kinking the material, using tongs, and sets stops on the table, using handtools, and cuts the work piece to a specified length, using a circular saw or power shears. The rod puller also rolls finished lengths into a trough for cooling. May stamp grade, alloy mixture, and batch number on each work piece.

Find employment in this job by searching your local newspaper 🗞, telephone book ☎, or the Web 💻 under: Pipe, Pipe Bending, Pipe Contractors, Pipe Fittings, Tube Fittings, Wire Forms-Manufacturers, Wire Manufacturers, Wire Products, Wire Products-Wholesale and Manufacturers.

Scratcher

A scratcher granulates color mixes for use in hard-surface floor covering. The scratcher adjusts roll clearance and speed of the scratcher motor to attain required particle size, using handtools, and starts a scratch mill, and positions pans under the discharge trough to receive the granulated mix from the scratch mill. The scratcher records the number of pans filled along with the color and pattern data on tickets and affixes the tickets to loaded handtrucks. The scratcher also pushes handtrucks to a storage area, weighs and adds oils or other liquid materials to the mix as required or may be alternately designated according to task performed as a color receiver.

Find employment in this job by searching your local newspaper 🗞, telephone book ☎, or the Web 💻 under: Floor Materials-Retail, Floor Materials-Wholesale and Manufacturers, Floor-Contractors and Builders, Floors-Industrial, Floors-Laying, Floors-Refinishing and Resurfacing.

Screw Supervisor

This title is sometimes reserved for the director on a porn set, but only unofficially. Officially, a screw supervisor supervises and coordinates activities of workers engaged in fabricating watch screws.

Find employment in this job by searching your local newspaper 🖥, telephone book ☎, or the Web 💻 under: Jewelers-Manufacturers, Jewelry-Designers, Manufacturing-General, Watches, Watchmens-Lock and Systems.

Skull Grinder

Picks up split and brained hogs' heads and holds their nasal passages against a revolving emery wheel to clean out dirt and removes dirt from their ear passages. When done, the skull grinder throws the hogs' heads in a container.

Find employment in this job by searching your local newspaper 🖥, telephone book ☎, or the Web 💻 under: Butchers, Farms, Livestock Dealers, Slaughterhouses.

Slasher

A slasher cuts plastic materials to specified lengths, mounts rolls of plastic sheeting material on a cutting-machine holding stand, using a hoist, sets cutting guides and moves a knife to slice materials being unreeled across the table and examines the sheets for defects and scraps and weighs unusable ones.

i Find employment in this job by searching your local newspaper 📰, telephone book ☎, or the Web 💻 under: Plastics-Fabricating, Plastics-Forming, Plastics and Plastic Products-Machined, Plastics-Products-Finished-Retail, Plastics-Products-Finished-Wholesale and Manufacturers.

Who's Your Daddy? How and Where to Go to Be a Sperm Donor

Eligibility

You are eligible to become a sperm donor:

1. If you are between the ages of eighteen and forty,
2. You are in good health,
3. You do not have a history of chronic health problems and have not been exposed to or infected with HIV, hepatitis, syphilis, genital herpes, or genital warts.

In order to be approved as a donor your sperm must be evaluated for fertility — if it's fertile you move to the next step.

A typical screening process usually takes a few weeks, sometimes up to eight weeks. During the screening period, you'll make regular visits to the sperm bank, each of which takes between fifteen minutes and an hour. You provide semen samples by masturbating in a private room and then your fertility is evaluated. If your semen is acceptable you will then be asked to complete a family health history form, listing any physical or mental conditions that preexist. You are screened for HIV and other sexually transmitted diseases for which you'll be asked to provide urine and blood samples in addition to more semen samples. If nothing else, look at it as a free health screening!

Commitment

Some programs require a one-year commitment with a minimum of one visit per week — sometimes two! (Eat your Wheaties!!!) Programs also ask that you refrain from ejaculating for 48 hours prior to providing samples.

Compensation

Once accepted into a donor program, pay varies from $50-$100 for every sample that meets a sperm bank's minimum sperm count requirement. Payment can also include retroactive pay for the samples provided during the screening period and a sign-on bonus! Sometimes an exit bonus is paid. Again, check with the clinic in your area. Also, if you refer someone who is accepted, most clinics offer finder's fees.

Sperm Banks

California Cryobank
Internet: www.cryobank.com/
Openness policy
Online donor catalog. Corporate Headquarters:
1019 Gayley Avenue
Los Angeles, CA 90024
Phone: 800-231-3373, 310-443-5244
Fax: 310-443-5258

Fertility Center of California
Internet: www.fertilityctr.com/
Sex selection
1125 East 17th Street, W-120
Santa Ana, CA 92701
Phone: 714-953-5683

Options National Fertility Register
Internet: www.fertilityoptions.com/
e-mail: info@fertilityoptions.com
Various levels of identity disclosure
PO Box 6209
Garden Grove, CA 92846
Phone: 800-786-1786
Fax: 562-404-5043

Pacific Fertility Center
Internet: www.pfmc.com/
e-mail: pfpc@pfmc.com

Pacific Reproductive Services
Internet: www.hellobaby.com
e-mail: pacrepro@slip.net
When child reaches age 18
Offers "Willing-to-be-Known" donors
Lesbian and single-women friendly
Offices in San Francisco and Pasadena, California
Phone: 415-487-2288

Rainbow Flag Health Services
Internet: www.gayspermbank.com/
e-mail: leland@gayspermbank.com
When child reaches age 3 months
Actively recruits gay and bisexual donors
*The only sperm bank to tell the mother who the donor is
when the child is three months old*
Oakland, CA
Phone: 510-763-SPERM (7737)

The Sperm Bank of California
Internet: www.thespermbankofca.org/
When child reaches age 18
Offers "Identity-Release" donors, Lesbian and single-women friendly, First nonprofit sperm bank in the US
2115 Milvia Street, 2nd Floor
Berkeley, CA 94704-1112
Phone: 510-841-1858
Fax: 510-841-0332

ZyGen Laboratory
Internet: www.zygen.com/
e-mail: csdirector@zygen.com
Sex selection
16742 Stagg Street, Suite 105
Van Nuys, CA 91406
Phone: 800-255-7242, 818-988-2500
Fax: 818-988-2734

CryoGam Colorado, Inc.
Internet: www.cryogam.com/
1805 E. 18th Street
Loveland, CO 80538
Phone: 800-473-9601
Fax: 303-667-9906

University of Connecticut Health Center (Xytex Affiliate)
Farmington, Connecticut
Phone: 860-679-3460

Cryobanks International
Internet: www.cryo-intl.com
e-mail: clientservices@cryo-intl.com
270 S. Northlake Blvd., #1012
Altamonte Springs, FL 32701
Phone: 800-869-8608, 407-834-8333
Fax: 407-834-3533

Florida Institute for Reproductive Medicine (Xytex Affiliate)
Jacksonville, FL
Phone: 904-399-5620

Reproductive Health Associates (Xytex Affiliate)
Clearwater, FL
Phone: 813-572-5300

Paces Cryobank and Infertility Services
Internet: www.pacescryobank.com/
e-mail: glminc@mindspring.com
2205 Corporate Plaza Pkwy
Atlanta, GA 30080
Phone: 770-850-1270
Fax: 770-850-1280

Xytex Corporation
Internet: www.xytex.com/
e-mail: xytex@xytex.com
Online catalog.
1100 Emmett St.
Augusta, GA 30904
Phone: 800-277-3210, 706-733-0130
Fax: 706-736-9270

Atlanta office:
730 Peachtree Street, NE
Suite 1145
Atlanta, GA 30308
Phone: 404-881-0426

LaVista Reproductive Services (Xytex Affiliate)
Atlanta, GA
Phone: 770-491-1304

UIC University Andrology Laboratory
Internet: www.uic.edu/com/mcsr/androlab/donor.htm
The Urology Clinic at the University of Illinois at Chicago
Medical Center
840 South Wood Street
University Center for Urology and Male Reproduction
900 North Michigan Avenue Annex, Suite 1420
Phone: 312-996-7713 or 312-996-5720

Follas Laboratories, Inc.
Internet: www.follas.com/
e-mail: info@follas.com
7750 Zionsville Road, Suite 450
Indianapolis, IN 46268
Phone: 317-879-2800, 800-969-0852

The Fertility Institute
Internet: www.fertilityinstitute.com/
e-mail: info@fertilityinstitute.com
6020 Bullard Avenue
New Orleans, LA 70128
Phone: 800-433-9009, in LA 800-375-0048, 504-246-BABY

New England Cryogenic
Internet: www.necryogenic.com
e-mail: info@necryogenic.com
665 Beacon Street, Suite 301
Boston, MA 02215
Phone: 617-262-3311, 800-991-4999
Fax: 617-262-1234
Their London office e-mail address for information about
shipping to the UK is info@cordbloodbank.co.uk.

Abbott Northwestern Hospital Andrology Laboratory
Minneapolis, MN
Phone: 612-863-4115

Cryogenic Laboratories, Inc.
Internet: www.cryolab.com/
e-mail: info@cryolab.com
1944 Lexington Avenue North
Roseville, MN 55113
Phone: 800-466-2796, 612-489-8000
Fax: 612-489-8989

Northwest Andrology and Cryobank, Inc.
Internet: www.nwcryobank.com/
e-mail to: nwcryo@ior.com
*Will ship to home without doctor consent. Good for those do-
ing at-home insemination.*
2825 Fort Missoula Road
Physicians Center #1, Suite 121
Missoula, MT 59804
Phone: 406-549-0958

University of Nebraska Medical Center
Human Genetics Laboratories
Omaha, NE
Phone: 402-559-5070

Biogenetics
Internet: www.sperm1.com/
PO Box 1290
Mountainside, NJ 07092
Phone: 800-637-7776

Idant Laboratories Division (DAXOR)
Internet: www.idant.com/
350 Fifth Avenue, Suite 7120
New York, NY 10118
Phone: 212-244-0555
Fax: 212-244-0806

Park Avenue Fertility
35 Park Avenue
New York, NY 10016
Phone: 212-779-1608

Repro Lab, Inc
Internet: www.reprolabinc.com/
e-mail: info@reprolabinc.com
336 East 30th Street
New York, NY 10016
Phone: 212-779-3988
Fax: 212-779-3908

Rochester Regional Cryobank
Rochester, NY
Phone: 800-321-7412

North Carolina Center for Reproductive Medicine (Xytex Affiliate)
Cary, NC
Phone: 919-233-1680

Cryobiology
Columbus, OH
Phone: 800-359-4375

Oregon Health Sciences University
Internet: www.fertilityoregon.com
e-mail: fertclin@ohsu.edu (clinic),
e-mail: fertlab@ohsu.edu (lab)
1750 S.W. Harbor Way, Suite l00
Portland, OR 97201
Phone: 503-494-8261
Fax: 503-418-3708 (clinic), 503-418-3767 (lab)

Pennsylvania Andrology and Fertility Center
Wyomissing, PA
Phone: 610-373-7668

Baylor College of Medicine
Houston, TX
Phone: 713-798-4001

Fairfax Cryobank
Internet: www.fairfaxcryobank.com/
e-mail: cryobank@givf.com
A Division of GIVF
3015 Williams Drive, #110
Fairfax, VA 22031
Phone: 800-338-8407, 703-698-3976
Fax: 703-698-3933

Scandinavian Cryobank
Internet: www.scandinaviancryobank.com
e-mail: info@scandinaviancryobank.com
730 N 83rd Street
Seattle, WA 98103
Phone: 206-784-0057, 866-366-6777
Fax: 425-952-1206
Extended profiles with answers to questions in essay form.
Scandinavian Cryobank is an American sperm bank based in
Seattle that specializes in worldwide delivery of cryopre-
served donor sperm from Scandinavian donors.

Washington Fertility Study Center
Washington, DC
Phone: 202-333-3100

Stoner

"Hey Dude!"

A stoner smoothes the enameled surface of jewelry articles
by using an abrasive stone. The stoner fastens jewelry articles
in a wooden chuck (jeweler's block), rubs a moist abrasive
stone across the articles to remove excess enamel and produce
a smooth surface, and brushes or washes the articles to remove

loose particles. A stoner may also remove excess enamel, using a buffing machine.

(i) Find employment in this job by searching your local newspaper 🗞, telephone book ☎, or the Web 💻 under: Jewelers-Manufacturers, Jewelry-Designers, Jewelry-Repair.

You'd Never Think
Stripping Credentials
Could Launch a Political Career, But They Can!

Ex-Stripper Earning Catcalls as Town Mayor: The Koleen Brooks Story

She caused an uproar by going from local stripper to the Mayor of Georgetown, Colorado, supposedly smoked pot and exposed herself in public and even posed for *Playboy*. Don't be surprised if you see Koleen Brooks on TV either, and rumor has it she's received film offers, too! Oh yeah, and she runs a hair salon called Dare 2 Be Different in her spare time. Pretty impressive when your resume highlights include: Exotic dancer at Shotgun Willies for 15 years.

"There couldn't be a better soap opera," Brooks said, describing the brouhaha between city officials and herself. Since she was elected mayor, she has been accused by the straight-laced establishment of everything from baring her breasts in public to hiring a hit man to get rid of a police officer.

About her breasts, Koleen says, "I paid a lot of money for these pretty things," she said, referring to her breast enlargement surgery.

Many women have stripper success stories to tell. For years women have used their stripping income to put themselves through college and started their own businesses. Here are some tips to getting started in stripping. From the Web site *The Stripper-FAQ: How to Become an Exotic Dancer,* here's what you need to break into the business and build that political resume!

Tools of the Trade

Other than your body, which is covered in the next section, the tools of the stripping trade are clothing, makeup, and shoes. As with any other trade, it never pays to buy cheap tools — they don't work well, they break and you'll just have to replace them anyway.

Heels are your first purchase. Minimum height is three inches — anything shorter and your gut will stick out and your legs will look like tree trunks. Look for a shoe with a plastic one-piece sole and heel. Shoes with the leather and wood heels are much more elegant but after the second night of dancing on them the heels tend to flex too much and put a lot of stress on your knees and back. Open toes tend to be more comfortable but if you're going to wear them you have to make sure your toenails are painted and trimmed. Putting no-slip rubber pads on the bottom of the shoe is a good idea — it prevents embarrassing falls on slippery stages.

Bottoms come in a few different varieties: Choose according to your tastes, club rules, etc. Almost all clubs require thongs. Some topless clubs have rules against g-strings (string sides and back) because they tend to not provide enough coverage to comply with local laws.

Girls who try dancing in underwear or a swimsuit bottom always look tacky. Buy the right kind.

Some clubs don't care what kind of dress you wear — lots of girls wear neon spandex micro minis, etc. Other clubs called "gown clubs" have more strict rules and generally require these sort of slutty evening gowns. These gowns, like the bottoms, need to be custom made or ordered — nothing from the department store will cut it. Another important note — NEVER ever wear an asymmetrical dress (hem cut at an angle or one shoulder strap). As most people know, men subconsciously look at certain physical attributes as signs of good genetics and a desirable partner — boobs, hips, etc. They also look for something anthropologists call "Bilateral Symmetry," which means that your arms and legs are the same length, your torso is straight, etc. An asymmetrical dress throws this off. It may look nice but you can actually chart the drop in earnings on a night-to-night basis.

Hair. Neck down it's all gotta go. Leave a little patch on top. Even if you're only dancing topless you have to keep it pretty clear. It looks really gross when little strands of hair stick out from the side of your bottoms. Most girls wax, get electrolysis, or have it lasered away. Keep up with it. Stubble is a definite no-no and shaving several days a week causes irritation and ingrown hair — laser or electrolysis are definitely recommended.

Make up is pretty easy — most girls already know how to do that. Some clubs have their own makeup artists — they generally do a good job but tend to make all the girls look the same. A vital tool of the trade is body makeup. This is used to cover any blemishes that you might have on your body. If your club does a lot of pole or floor work, you will need body makeup, as that kind of dancing causes a lot of leg bruising.

A Stripper's Body Is a Stripper's Cash Register

What kind of shape you're in makes a bigger difference in your earnings than anything else. An hour of exercise a day can mean $200 more a night. It's important that you understand that your body is how you earn a living; as such you have to take very good care of it. In the world of strip clubs the name of the game is low body fat. Sure some men like extra padding, but no one likes cheese. It's an unfortunate truth, but the slimmer you are the more money you will make. You don't have to be fashion model skinny but you do have to be tight if you expect to make good money. Yoga or weight training is ideal for the kind of look that men like.

The most effective weight training exercises for woman are squats, lunges and stiff-leg or sumo deadlifts. None of these lifts should be done on machines — free weights only. Machines are not nearly as effective. Train heavy and train hard. Yoga and dancing are both very catabolic activities (they break down muscle tissue). You will not get bulky.

A typical daily routine should consist of:

Squats: 3 sets of 20 reps, 120 seconds rest between sets.
Stiff-leg deadlifts: 3 sets of 10 reps, 120 seconds rest between sets.
Rest 5 minutes
Dumbbell lunges: 4 sets of 12 reps, 90 seconds rest between sets
Hanging crunches: 4 sets 90 seconds rest between sets

The squats should be to failure; it should be VERY hard to hit 20. Like having a baby hard. Squats will make a bigger change in your physique than anything else. When you do your yoga and running, do it in the morning on an empty stomach. If you have a real fat problem, an hour of running or jump rope a day before breakfast with a low/no carb diet can take off a lot of fat in a short period of time.

One of the problems with maintaining relatively low levels of body fat is that there is no way to have "spot" fat loss. It's all or nothing. As you lose the fat off your butt and thighs you also lose your breasts — often as much as a cup size. This is the reason that many dancers choose to have breast augmentation. There are lots of men who rail against implants, about how they don't like them and how they can always tell the difference, but that's bullshit. The only time they can tell is if it's a bad implant job; since they think the good jobs are real, they assume that all implants look bad. Girls estimate an additional 20% in earnings after they got their augmentation and that most men seem to find them much, much more attractive.

Different diets work for different people. Regardless of what you choose, it has to be something you can stay on permanently. You can't just diet when you think you're getting fat, as a dancer you have to maintain a consistently low level of body fat. For me carbs are the problem. Avoid low-fat foods or at least read the labels carefully, they tend to have a lot of sugar and nothing gets you fat faster than sugar — not even fat. Try to break your meals down into several small ones — this helps you metabolize your food better. Avoid high-carb meals and if you're going to cheat do it early in the day.

Trying Out for the Part

Your first and most important concern is to find a suitable club. It needs to be a place where you feel safe and comfortable. It doesn't matter how good the money is, if the place makes you feel bad about yourself you'll be miserable working there. Go to the Ultimate Strip Club List at http://www.tuscl.com/ and look for clubs in your area. The reviews will give you a very good idea of whether it's a place you want to work. For example, if the guy says, "Wow, it was great. This girl let me feel her up," it's obviously not a place you want to work. Looking for a good club is like looking for any other job — you want to get the most money for the least amount of work.

So what kind of money will you be making? If you're dancing for shift pay in a blue collar "titty bar" you'll make about

$150 a night. A go-go or "cage" dancer at a regular nightclub might make $200 a night but she'll be dancing almost all night. Some girls might prefer that — you don't have to work for tips or talk to the guys. A girl dancing for tips and drink commission in a nude club makes between $200 to $600. A pretty, well-spoken girl who knows the business will make between $400 to $800 at a topless "gown" club. (Gown club refers to a club where the girls wear gowns and the clientele is more upscale.) A feature dancer who has done some magazine and movie work might make $1500 a night. These numbers vary from state to state. It also depends on the club, your verbal skills and your looks — in that order. Believe it or not the girls who make the most money stripping are rarely the prettiest. It's the ones who know how to tell the guys what they want to hear who make the real money.

There's no way around it, the first time you get on stage you're going to be scared out of your wits. DON'T have a drink to "calm your nerves." Drinking on the job is a really bad idea; it can let you permit guys to take liberties you would not otherwise allow.

When you're ready, just show up at the club and say you'd like an audition, be nice to whoever is working the door — they frequently screen girls for the managers. They may ask you to come back on another night but they normally just put you on one of the side stages. One of the managers will watch you dance for a few songs then talk to you a little bit to make sure you've got a good attitude, etc.

As far as dancing is concerned a lot depends on the club. You have to see the way the other strippers dance. Some clubs don't allow floor or pole work, while in others they do all that plus shower and lesbian shows. Even if you're straight, the lesbian shows can be a lot of fun, but they are never mandatory. Most clubs work on a standard three-song set. That means for the first song when you're on stage you have all your clothes on, the second, you remove something and for the last you wear either nothing or just a thong depending on whether it's a nude or topless club. There is not a whole lot to dancing. You do not need lessons or to buy a video. Just watch what the other girls are doing, you'll pick it up in a few minutes. Just avoid anything showy or dramatic until you know how to do it right. Before you audition I would suggest trying out some of your moves in front of a mirror then getting some constructive criticism from a guy (they can be very helpful and are usually delighted to assist). Once you get to know the other dancers they will generally help out and show you some of the trickier moves. Guys appreciate a good dancer but seldom buy dances from a girl based on her dancing ability. You're better off spending the time working out and improving your physique.

Making Money

At most clubs you walk around and ask the customers if they'd like a private dance (or lap dance depending on the club). Some clubs just have stage dancing. Often there is a private area that you can go to for a dance. The most important thing to do when you're dancing is to SMILE AND MAKE EYE CONTACT. Nothing turns a guy off faster than a dancer strolling around the stage bored while staring vacantly off into space. Try to make each guy you're dancing for think he's the ONLY guy you're dancing for. This is how the pros make the big bucks.

At many clubs a significant part of your nightly earnings comes from dances. Most of the time the customer will pay for you to sit and talk with them as well. Guys vary a lot but it's always important to be attentive. Nobody likes to feel like they're being ignored. Most guys are pretty nice and easy to talk to. Provided you're a good listener and act interested, it's no problem.

It's important you have respect for the money you receive, so much money changes hands that girls often forget what it represents. Let's say your customer earns $40,000 a year after taxes — probably about average income for a strip club patron in NYC. That works out to around $20 an hour. If a customer sits with you and you make $100, that's five hours of his time. If a handyman came to your house and fixed things for five hours you'd say "thank you" right? Always thank the customer and make sure he knows you mean it. Even if $100 doesn't seem like a lot of money to you, to the average customer it is.

One last thing, don't screw with the guys' heads. It's not cool, and you can make money without doing it. After a few repetitions it gets very fake and you just come off as a greedy gold digger. If you want customers to treat you with respect you should treat them with respect. If they are disrespectful just walk away; there is no reason for you to sink to their level. There are more than enough good men who will pay you to sit, talk ,and laugh with them and when you dance they will treat you like a goddess. As customers they deserve your courtesy and if they don't respect you in return they don't deserve to have you spend time with them.

How To Manage Your Financial Portfolio: For Strippers Only

The minute you start dancing the clock is ticking. There are a limited number of years in which to make as much money as you can. Most dancers retire around 28. If you're starting when you're 18 that gives you ten years in which to make as much as you can and then get out. Chances are you will never again be able to make as much per day as you do while dancing. Make the most of it.

There are two kinds of dancers, subsistence and capital dancers. A subsistence dancer just works enough to get by, maybe a few days a week, saves little and is always in a financial crisis. I see these girls panicking to get enough dances to pay rent the next day but by the next week they are back to partying, doing drugs, buying expensive clothes and generally pissing away every dime they earn. Their plans for the future are vague at best and even though they claim to realize they can't dance forever they seldom save and invest their money or invest in an education. These girls get out of the business no better than they started and spend the rest of their lives getting their ass pinched in menial, low paying jobs.

A capital dancer dances as an investment. If you work hard you can make a great deal of money dancing.

When you see that money in your hand it just doesn't seem real, and when you keep seeing it night after night it seems like the supply will be endless. It's not; you need to put away the largest portion you can. Not just a 10% or so, but 30% or 40%.

If you can just keep it under control for a few years you can have that stuff for the rest of your life — long after you're done dancing. Live within your means; base your spending around not what you make dancing but what you would make at a good entry-level job. Get a good, reliable car but you don't need that giant SUV or zippy sports car. Make sure your lease or car loan doesn't rely on a dancer's level of income to pay it. Same goes for the rent or mortgage. It's very easy to fall on heels and break an ankle or tear up your knee — happens all the time. You could be out of work for weeks or even months. You don't want to be buried under a mountain of bills. I suggest buying at least basic health insurance but if you don't you will need at least enough savings to pay for emergencies.

So what to do with the money you save? Well, set enough aside to pay for all of your expenses — food, housing, tuition, utilities, car, whatever for four months. This is your emergency fund, put it in your savings account and don't spend it. The rest you should invest. As a dancer you're looking to invest for the long term — at least five years and probably ten. Mutual funds are low maintenance and are well suited for this. I strongly advise against investing in individual stocks. Despite all tales of buying low and selling high at the end of the year very few people are able to make money off buying and selling individual stocks. Stick with mutual funds, they are safer and more reliable (at least for the novice investor).

Stroker

Billy Squier said it best: "Now everybody have you heard, if you're in the game, then the stroke's the word..."

A stroker operates a stroke-belt sanding machine to smooth flat surfaces or edges of wood furniture stock. The stroker turns handwheels to set the tension of the belt, adjusts the machine table height, and limits the stroke of the pressure shoe, according to the thickness and length of stock. The stroker presses switches to start the sander, and positions the wood-stock to be sanded on the machine table located under the sanding belt. The stroker presses levers to lower the pressure shoe onto the sanding belt and to force the belt against the surface of the stock to sand, then pushes or pulls the table to move the stock under the belt to smooth its entire surface. The stroker feels sanded articles to ascertain smoothness, cleans machines, using an airhose and rags and replaces worn sanding belts. The stroker also presses the belt against stock with pressure blocks to bevel corners and edges of stock, or to smooth flat surfaces of ornamental stock.

i—Find employment in this job by searching your local newspaper 📰, telephone book ☎, or the Web 💻 under: Furniture Dealers and Custom Builders, Furniture Repair and Refinishing, Furniture Stripping, Furniture-Wholesale and Manufacturers, Wood Finishing, Wood Products-Manufacturers, Woodworking.

Sulky Driver

A sulky driver drives a horse-drawn, two-wheel sulky in a harness race. The sulky driver first studies the performance records of competing horses to plan a race strategy. While racing, the sulky driver controls the speed of his or her horse in specific sections of racetrack, applying knowledge of harness racing to determine when to challenge for the lead of race. The sulky driver may also train harness racing horses or direct the activities of workers involved in grooming, training, feeding, stabling, handling and transporting harness race horses.

i—Find employment in this job by searching your local newspaper 📰, telephone book ☎, or the Web 💻 under: Horse and Carriage Rental, Stables.

Erection Shop Supervisor

"Yep, that'll do."
"Nope. You need Viagra!"

A supervisor of an erection shop oversees and coordinates the activities of workers engaged in fitting, welding, and riveting railroad car components, such as beams, center sills, crossbearers, sides, ends, and roofing, to make the car framework. The supervisor of an erection shop also performs other supervisory duties as necessary.

(*i*) Find employment in this job by searching your local newspaper 📰, telephone book ☎, or the Web 💻 under: Contractors-General, Railroad Contractors, Railroad Equipment and Supplies, Welding.

The Low-Down on **Taxidermy**

Taxidermy is a general term describing the many methods of reproducing life-like representations of animals for permanent display. In some cases, the actual skin (including the fur, feathers or scales) of the specimen is preserved and mounted over an artificial armature. In other cases, the specimen is reproduced completely with man-made materials.

The modern practice of taxidermy incorporates many crafts, such as carpentry, woodworking, tanning, molding and casting, but it also requires artistic talent, including the art of sculpture, painting and drawing. In a modern deer head mount, for example, the only natural parts of the animal used are the antlers and the skin. All of the other organs and tissues are recreated with man-made materials. The eyes are made from glass, the eyelids are sculpted from clay, the soft tissues of the nose and mouth are sculpted from epoxy or wax, and the "form" (which incorporates the anatomy of each muscle and vein) is made from polyurethane foam.

Today, some taxidermy mounts (most notably saltwater fish) do not contain *any* parts of the animal at all. They are completely recreated from manmade materials. This is ideal for catch-and-release anglers, who can release their gamefish unharmed, and can still have a life-sized trophy produced from a good color photo and measurements.

Works of taxidermy are displayed in museums, educational institutions, businesses, restaurants, and homes. There are many different methods for producing mounts (or recreations) of different species.

Network with hunting clubs and pet fanatics to get the most for your work. Below and on the next page are the going rates.

Wall mounts and life size:

SPECIES	FULL SHOULDER	LIFE SIZE
Antelope	$400	$1800
Bear- Black (up to 5 ft.)	$425	$1800
Bear- Black (5 ft. to 6 ft.)	$425	$1950
Bear - Black (over 6 ft.)	$425	$2200
Bear - Black ½ body	N/A	$900-1200
Bear - Grizzly	N/A	$2900
Bear - Brown	N/A	$3500
Bear - Polar	N/A	$3900
Boar open mouth	$475	$1995
Buffalo (Bison)	$800	$6100
Caribou	$475	$3500
Deer	$350	$1900
Deer - Wall Pedestal	$400	N/A
Deer - Sitka	$375	$1995
Deer - Pedestal	$425 Plus Base	N/A
Elk	$500	$3500
Fox	$200	$425
Goats	$475	$2200
Moose	$775	$4500
Mountain Lion	N/A	$1800
Mountain Goat	$475	$2200
Mule Deer	$375	$1800
Musk Ox	$1100	$3800
Raccoon	$275	$425
Sheep (Dall, Stone, Bighorn, etc.)	$475	$2200
Wolf	N/A	$1700

Small animals:

SPECIES	LIFE SIZE MOUNTS
Beaver	$375
Badger	$400
Bobcat	$425
Coyote	$475
Fox	$425
Ground Hog	$375
Jack Rabbit	$325
Mink or Ferret	$325
Rabbit	$275
Raccoon	$425
Otter	$425
Squirrel	$160
Snake	$9 per inch, $100 minimum
Wolverine	$700

Birds:

SPECIES	STANDING	FLYING
Ducks	$150	$175
Doves	$150	$175
Geese	$185	$200
Grouse	$150	$175
Pheasant	$170	$195
Quail	$150	$170
Swans w/ permit	$400	$490
Turkey	$375	$425
Turkey Full strut on base	$425	N/A

Fish:

Skin Mount	$12.00 per inch
Reproduction	$12.00 per inch

Trophy Wife

A trophy wife is a woman who is much younger than her husband. She's usually a second wife or wife taken during a man's mid-life crisis. He shows her off as proof he's still got it! She is constantly rewarded with expensive gifts and dinners and all a trophy wife needs to do is look good. How to do it? Hook a guy on the rebound (while his defenses are down) or go online and surf the 40-50-year-old range (typical male mid-life crisis age), or if you can stomach elderly men, even better (Anna Nicole Smith made a killing). Tony Randall, Luciano Pavarotti and Larry King all married women half their ages, so there's definitely potential in this line of business!!!

Trucker's Eyes

To work in the capacity of a trucker's eyes is to know all the highways and byways of your state. If you're good with maps, roads and shortcuts, acting as a trucker's eyes is right up your alley! What a trucker's eyes does is meet truckers at the state border and drive in front of them, guiding them to their desti-nation or through the state as necessary. Many truckers and trucking companies hire people as trucker's eyes because it saves time for the trucker and, in areas with heavy construc-tion, the trucker's eyes can get truckers through on time by leading them down little known roads to avert gridlock.

All you need is a valid driver's license, a CB and a handle! (That's a CB name, e.g. The Bandit.)

Find employment in this job by searching your local newspaper 📰, telephone book ☎, or the Web 🖥 under: Trucking-General, Trucking-Heavy Hauling, Trucking-Liquid or Dry Bulk, Trucking-Motor Freight, Trucking-Refrigerator, Trucking-Transportation Brokers.

Tumor Registrar

A tumor registrar compiles and maintains the records of hospital patients treated for cancer, to provide data for physicians and research studies, utilizing a tumor registry data system. The tumor registrar reviews hospital records to identify and compile patient data for use in cancer management programs and to comply with government regulations. The tumor registrar reviews patients' medical records, abstracts and codes information, such as demographic characteristics, history and extent of disease, diagnostic procedures and treatment, and enters the data into a computer. The tumor registrar contacts discharged patients, their families, and physicians to maintain the registry with follow-up information, such as quality of life and length of survival of cancer patients and prepares statistical reports, narrative reports and graphic presentations of tumor registry data for use by hospital staff, researchers, and other users of registry data. The tumor registrar may also supervise subordinate tumor registry staff and may also be known as a tumor registry manager.

Find employment in this job by searching your local newspaper 📧, telephone book ☎, or the Web 🖥 under: Cancer Support Services, Cancer Treatment Centers, Hospitals, Medical Centers.

Umbrella Tipper

Type 1: This umbrella tipper handsews umbrella covers to frames. The umbrella tipper tacks the umbrella cover to the ribs along the seams and sews the corners to the tips of the ribs. The umbrella tipper then sews ties to the outside of the cover to hold the umbrella when folded.

Type 2: This umbrella tipper attaches metal or plastic tips to the corners of prestitched umbrella covers. The umbrella tipper positions tips in a machine fixture and holds the corner of the cover in position to receive the tips. The umbrella tipper may also press the pedal of the machine to release tips and secure tips to corners of the cover or sew tips in place with needle and thread.

Find employment in this job by searching your local newspaper 📰, telephone book ☎, or the Web 💻 under: Clothing-Men's-Wholesale and Manufacturers, Clothing-Women's and Misses'-Wholesale and Manufacturers, Fabrics-Wholesale and Manufacturers, Seamstresses, Sewing Contractors.

Unemployment Collector, Professional: The 52/26 Plan for Free Time and a Paycheck

Who Can Do It?

Eligibility differs from state to state, but in general you're eligible if you've been discharged from a job for any reason and have at least a year of employment to your record (in which taxes have been taken out). If you have quit a job you may still be eligible. (I have a friend who did this.) If that's the case, a formal hearing will be called to determine your entitlement to benefits. If it was a bad job with poor working conditions, chances are you'll be able to collect.

How Does It Work?

If you're part of a large corporate downsizing, as I was prior to writing this, filing is a cinch! All you need to do is call your local unemployment office (you can find listings under your state's Department of Labor Web site or in the phone book). Your Human Resources Manager may also provide you with this information. If you have a pink slip, all you need to do is present it at your local unemployment office and fill out some paperwork and the ball will begin to roll. If you have been fired, you will need to meet with a Department of Labor representative and explain the details of your discharge. They, in turn, will contact your former employer and see if they feel you should not receive unemployment compensation for any reason. Unless you did something truly horrible to your former employer, you're usually eligible. Now, some people make unemployment a career. They call it the 52/26 plan: You work a year (52 weeks)/you collect unemployment for 6 months (26 weeks).

Once you've called in, reported your discharge, or had a hearing at which you were determined eligible for unemployment, all you need to do is call in once a week and answer a few questions. You call either on a Sunday or a Monday and receive a check within two business days of your call. Most labor departments have an automated system, so as long as you answer the questions correctly you can continue to file for the duration of your 26 weeks. You should, however, keep track of all jobs you apply for in that time in case of a random check to ensure you are actively seeking work. Here are the questions you'll have to answer. (Again, this may differ slightly from state to state. The questions below are from the State of Connecticut Department of Labor.)

In the previous week:

1. Were you able to work, available for work and actively seeking full-time work?

2. Did you refuse an offer of work or rehire, quit a job or get discharged from a job?
3. Did you receive your first payment from Social Security or a pension which you have not already reported or was there a change in the amount previously reported?
4. Did you start school, college or training, which you have not already reported to the Department of Labor?
5. Did you receive vacation pay, severance pay or workers' compensation benefits, not previously reported?
6. Did you work full-time or part-time for an employer or in self-employment or return to full-time work for the week ending last Saturday, which you have not already reported?
    (If you answer Yes to question 6 you are no longer eligible for unemployment compensation.)
7. Did you change your mailing address since you last filed a claim?

What Kind of Money Will I Receive?

The pay you receive for unemployment is based on the past four quarters (52 weeks) in which you were employed. The two highest paying quarters are averaged and the final result usually works out to half of what you were making per week while employed. If you have children you are allotted a Dependency Allowance. States may also impose a maximum weekly compensation rate that can lower your payments if your salary was higher than the average state salary. For example, I was making approximately $600 a week after taxes, benefits and my 401k contributions. My weekly unemployment check was for $365.

If the traditional work a year/only get a week or two weeks of vacation plan doesn't work for you — or maybe you're an artist and need time to devote to your craft — I highly recommend the 52/26 plan.

Wafer Cleaner

A wafer cleaner cleans the surfaces of semiconductor wafers after slicing or polishing. The wafer cleaner reviews work orders to determine processing steps, sets temperature controls on an automatic chemical cleaning machine or the sinks of a chemical cleaning station and places containers of semiconductor wafers into the drum of the cleaning machine or into the heated sinks of solutions in the cleaning station to remove dust, oil, wax, slurry, or debris from the surface of the wafers. The wafer cleaner also may load containers of wafers into a scrubbing machine that brushes and sprays contaminants from wafers and dries wafers. May tend a machine that dries wafers.

Find employment in this job by searching your local newspaper 🖳, telephone book ☎, or the Web 🖳 under: Chemicals, Chemicals-Manufacturers, Cleanrooms, Semiconductor Devices.

Weight Guesser

A weight guesser guesses the weight of patrons at an amusement park, carnival, or place of entertainment. The weight guesser attracts the attention of the passing public, vociferously announcing his or her game and skill, scrutinizes a patron's physique and makes an oral estimate of weight and invites patrons to stand on a scale or to sit in a seat attached to an industrial scale, usually forfeiting a prize if the weight guessed is not correct within two or three pounds. The weight guesser may demonstrate personal skill in guessing a patron's age, occupation, home state, or other related pertinent data.

i—Find employment in this job by searching your local newspaper 🗞, telephone book ☎, or the Web 💻 under: Amusement Places, Carnivals, Entertainment Agencies and Bureaus, Fairs, Festivals.

Whizzer

A whizzer spins felt hat bodies to remove excess water. To do this, the whizzer pulls the bodies over the hat-shaped holder of a machine or places the bodies in a basket, presses a button or depresses a pedal to start the holder or basket spinning, removing excess water from the bodies and releases a pedal to stop the machine and feels the hat bodies to ascertain dryness. Additionally, a whizzer may soak hat bodies in a waterproofing solution.

i—Find employment in this job by searching your local newspaper 🗞, telephone book ☎, or the Web 💻 under: Clothing-Men's-Wholesale and Manufacturers, Clothing-Women's and Misses'-Wholesale and Manufacturers, Fabric Treatment, Hats-Retail, Hats-Wholesale and Manufacturers.

Worm Grower

A worm grower breeds and raises earthworms for sale as fishing bait, garden soil conditioners, or as food for exotic fish and animals. The worm grower mixes sand, loam, and organic materials to make a growing medium for worms, fills growing tubs with the medium and adds water, plants mature worms in the growing media for breeding stock, spreads food materials over the surface of the medium and covers it with burlap, inspects food supply and moisture of the growing medium and adds water and food to maintain optimum breeding conditions for worms. When the time is right, the worm grower shovels the worm-laden medium onto a screen and shakes the screen to remove worms, places a specified number of worms into the sales container and scoops the required amount of growing medium into the container to sustain the worms and sells the earthworms to buyers. The worm grower may dry worms under heat lamps and grind and package them for sale as tropical fish food.

Find employment in this job by searching your local newspaper 📰, telephone book ☎, or the Web 💻 under: Fishing Bait, Fishing Consultants and Outfitters, Fishing Tackle-Dealers, Fishing Tackle-Wholesale and Manufacturers.

Wrestler

Becoming a professional wrestler is easier than one might think. You don't even need to be in shape — all you need is a gimmick. Maybe you're of exceptional size: large or small, exceptionally ugly or have some snappy lines, e.g., "Can you smell what The Rock is cookin'?"

Here is a list of training camps. They'll teach you the moves and the rest is up to you. Show up at wrestling events, send your resume to the WWE (no longer the WWF since too many people were mistakenly applying to the World Wildlife Fund!). It's all luck, but wrestling is a great gig if you're picked.

WCW Power Plant
404-351-4959

DCW School of Wrestling
811 West Reelfoot Ave. #99
Union City, TN 38261
901-885-8660
502-472-5704
800-278-2964
Internet: www.ken-tenn.net/diskwrestle/index.htm
e-mail: diskwrestle@ken-tenn.net

Bad Boy's House of Pain
169 St. Paul Street
Rochester, NY 14620
716-325-4590
e-mail: PRORESLR@aol.com

WWA Training Center
PO Box 862
Bourbonnais, IL 60914
815-933-3813
Internet: www.keynet.net/~wwa/train.html

Steel Domain Pro Wrestling Training Center
5643 W. Irving Park Road
Chicago, IL 60634
773-674-3888

NWA Hardcore Wrestling School
Box 2208
Hammond, IN 46323
219-641-5914

ECW House of Hardcore
516-586-7329

The Wrestling Academy
1530 Carroll Drive, Bldg. 106
Atlanta, GA 30318
404-473-9364
Attn: Mr. Joe Hamilton
This school supplies many graduate students to WCW.

Killer Kowalski School of Wrestling
Box 67
Reading, MA 01867

The Monster Factory
PO Box 345
Westville, NJ 08093
609-456-9181
Attn: Mr. Larry Sharpe
This school trained Bam Bam Bigelow, among many others.

Dom D'Nucci Training Academy
1730 Love Rd.
Freedom, PA 15042
Shane Douglas and Mankind are graduates.

Malenko Pro Wrestling Camp
12770 Woodtrail Blvd.
Tampa Bay, FL 33625
813-968-1359

Doug's Gym
2010½ Commerce St.
Attn: Mr. Jim Webbe
Dallas, TX 75201
Bruiser Brody and Dustin Rhodes trained here.

Slammer's Wrestling Gym
Attn: Verne Langdon
PO Box 1602
Studio City, CA 91614
818-897-6603
Internet: www.slammers.com

Ivan Koloff and Assoc. Wrestling School
PO Box 23360
Charlotte, NC 28227

Body Slammers Pro Wrestling Gym
PO Box 1472
Lima, OH 45802
Internet: www.angelfire.com/oh/ebbeskotte/index.html

Eddie Sharkey
Pro Wrestling America
6217 Chowen Ave. South
Edina, MN
612-926-1239
Trained Rick Rude, Syxx, Road Warriors, Jesse Ventura, and others.

The Wild Samoan Wrestling School
PO Box 251
Whitehall, PA 18052
717-459-1980
Internet: www.wildsamoan.com
Supplies graduates to the WWF.

What It Takes to Become a
Zamboni Driver

Zamboni drivers have been featured in beer commercials, hockey ads and, most notably, the 2002 Winter Olympics campaign. A Zamboni driver watches NHL hockey games for free, meets celebrities and gets paid to sit on his or her ass for 10 minutes a night! Those are the perks that 27-year-old Travis Larson enjoys as the Zamboni driver at the Xcel Energy Center in Saint Paul, Minnesota — that's the ice rink where the Minnesota Wild hockey team.

Travis wanted to be a Zamboni driver ever since he was eight years old when he started going to hockey games with his Dad. "I told my Dad I'm going to drive a Zamboni one day and ten years later I was driving the same machine I saw as a kid," says Travis. Here's a look at what it takes to be the guy who cleans the ice between periods at an NHL hockey game.

Travis started driving a Zamboni at smaller ice rinks for high school hockey games. He then went to a technical college in Minnesota where he studied Arena and Operations Management for two years. Soon after, Travis began driving the Zamboni for college hockey games. He became the Operations Manager of the Xcel Energy Center when the Minnesota Wild started playing hockey there during the 2000-2001 season.

"It's pretty neat when you're driving around the ice in front of 18,000 people. Fans stare at you and some wave, it's kinda cool," says Travis. He also likes meeting all the NHL stars that pass through the rink. Travis has met Wayne Gretzky and Steve Yzerman and he's also talked to the Dixie Chicks and the Barenaked Ladies when they've come to perform at the arena.

Travis says operating an NHL ice rink can sometimes mean working some pretty long hours. Making sure the ice is ready to go isn't always that easy. "Sometimes if you're not watching what you're doing, you can miss a turn. When people first start driving, learning to make the turns is probably the hardest thing," says Travis. You also have to know how much water to put on the ice. If you put too much water down, players will complain that the ice is too slow. A recent survey ranked the ice in the Xcel Energy Center as the eighth best in the league.

A Zamboni driver makes around $13 an hour, depending on which arena you work at, and a rise up to Operations Manager can mean between $40,000 - $50,000 a year.

Zig-Zag Stitcher

Not just any old stitcher, a zig-zag stitcher joins layers of material, seams garment parts, or attaches trim to garments. The zig-zag stitcher performs duties as described under the Sewing-Machine Operator, Regular Equipment Master title, such as operating machines equipped with different cams to sew decorative stitches, such as scallops. The zig-zag stitcher may also operate a variation of the zig-zag machine to join adjacent edges or flatten seams with decorative crisscross stitches and be designated a fagoting-machine operator.

Find employment in this job by searching your local newspaper 📧, telephone book ☎, or the Web 💻 under: Clothing-Men's-Wholesale and Manufacturers, Clothing-Women's and Misses'-Wholesale and Manufacturers, Designers-Apparel, Seamstresses, Sewing Contractors.

So, What Color Is Your Parachute Anyway?
Tips on Finding the Perfect Job

What Color Is Your Parachute: *A Practical Manual for Job-Hunters and Career-Changers* is the best-selling job-hunting book in the world with over seven million copies in print! This book has great advice about searching for jobs, interviewing, and finding your calling in life. So if all that works for "normal" jobs, why can't it work across the board? Maybe it's your destiny to become a dot etcher, a hair boiler, a whizzer or an anarchist.

Whether you're looking to become a marketing assistant or a macaroni press operator, here are some proven techniques from Richard N. Bolles' famous book.

The Traditional Job Hunt vs. The Life-Changing Job Hunt

When it is time for you to go job-hunting, you may think you have no choice. But you do. And that's because there is more than one kind of job-hunt. Two, in fact. And you get to choose which one you want to pursue.

The choice is between doing a traditional job-hunt, or doing a life-changing job-hunt. At some times in your life a traditional job-hunt will be all you need. At other times, a life-changing job-hunt, will look a lot more desirable. It just depends on what you're looking for, at that, or this, particular time in your life.

You get to choose. And you get to make this choice at least eight times in your life, because that's how many times the average person gets to go job-hunting — at a minimum. And each time you face the job-hunt, there's that choice again. "Shall I do just a traditional job-hunt? Or shall I embark on a life-changing job-hunt, this time?"

(So you can play it straight, remain unchallenged by remaining in the same job just in a different location, or you can go for it! Explore! Find a job you always wanted or never even dreamed of — corduroy-brushing, look out!!!)

The Traditional Job-Hunt

Its simplest form is found, not surprisingly, on the Internet. Even if you don't use the Internet, it's important for you to understand what's happening there. (Sadly, for all you hackers and slackers, the author points out in a later chapter that only 4% of all job-hunters land a job by using the Internet!) For, on the Internet, over the last ten years the traditional job-hunt has evolved into a form so simple you could almost call it "mechanical." Mechanical? Yes, on the Internet, the old "matching game" (matching employers' vacancies/ads/postings against job-hunters' resumes) is done not by a human but by a "robot," a piece of software called a "job-search agent" or a dozen other delicious names.

Here's how it works:

1.) *You prepare your resume.* Your resume is a summary of your experience, thus far, in the world of work. It describes where you've worked, what you accomplished there, and what skills you thereby have proved you have. It's essentially *an argument,* from your past, as to what you'll be able to accomplish for them (prospective employers) in the future.

2.) *You post your resume* on some Internet site that (a.) allows you to do that; (b.) has ads that are put up by employers on that same site; and (c.) has some "robot" or "job-search agent" that will compare your resume to all those employer ads.

3.) *When the "search while you sleep" program finds a match* of keywords (same keywords in the employer's ad as in your posted resume) it notifies you or the employer or both by e-mail that a match has been found. If you are interested, you contact the employer, or they contact you. The match is done by a piece of software.

Job-Hunt Statistics

Each year about 10% of all U.S. workers change careers (nearly 10 million workers). Of these:

- 5.3 million changed careers *voluntarily*, and in 7 out of 10 cases their income went up;
- 1.3 million changed careers *involuntarily*, because of the economy, and in 7 out of 10 cases, their income went down;
- 3.4 million changed careers for a *mixture* of voluntary and involuntary reasons (such as needing to go from part-time to full-time work, etc.).

Quick Fact: A survey conducted by the Roper Organization found that 45% of all U.S. workers said they would change their careers if they could.

The Life-Changing Job-Hunt

A job-hunt is just a job-hunt until we come to that point in our lives where we want to set our feet upon a new path. Then the traditional job-hunt — the *almost mechanical* matching of resume to vacancy — doesn't work very well at all. A life-changing job-hunt requires a different approach.

You're contemplating radically changing direction. This is called by various names. Sometimes it's called "Finding your Dream Job." Sometimes it's called "a career change." This author believes that most workers on the average just get bored. So why the hell not do something radical???

1.) *It begins with your defining just exactly what it is that you're looking for,* by way of change. There are six possibilities: (a.) You may be looking for a change in occupation, which is to say, job-title (and tasks). (b.) You may be looking for a change in field. (c.) You may be looking for a change in the kinds of people you work with. (d.) You may be looking for a change in your work environment. (e.) You may be looking for a kind of work that is more in keeping with the goals and values you have set for your life. (f.) You may be looking for a change in salary.

2.) *You must consider the three pathways to a career change* (in summary): (a.) You can do it in a single bound, jump from old career to new. (b.) You can do it one step at a time by changing your occupation first and then your field. (c.) You can do it one step at a time by first changing your field and then your occupation.

3.) *You must do a certain amount of homework on yourself, to define exactly what is the occupation and what is the field you want to go into, and then go find it.* You do this by defining:

What? You must decide just exactly what you have to offer the world.

Where? You must decide exactly where you want to use your skills (job field and geographic location).

How? You must go after the organizations that interest you the most, whether or not they are known to have a vacancy. (Bolles shows that two of the most successful ways of landing a job are knocking on doors and cold calling — you've got nothing to lose!)

The Office Space
Conclusion

The Demise of the Lunch Lady

Some off-beat jobs have fallen by the wayside in recent years. For example, Seal product sales plummeted in the early 2000s and lunch ladies have been replaced by corporations and pre-fab frozen meals. But, rest assured that there is a steady demand for blowers, load dispatchers, slashers and the other jobs listed in this book. And until every Mack out there is outfitted with GPS — trucker's eyes will remain in demand!

The market aside, what about us? The workers? With the "Me"-ism of the 80s taking over corporate America, many of us 30-somethings are starting to get the working class itch. Let's face it, if we're in it for 30 or more years until retirement, we may as well love what we do — or at least get a giggle out of it.

Do Nothing and Get Promoted

Office Space is a classic tale of how to do nothing and get promoted. (A highly recommended viewing!) So if you really have nothing in particular that's calling you, at least beat the system. I worked for years the honest way: never lying on a timesheet and never taking a sick day unless I was really sick, but no one really cared. My last employer laid off 75% of us and the one jerk who sat behind me downloading Aerosmith music and staring at Carmen Electra web sites all day remained employed!!! In fact, he got his own office shortly after that. I think he was onto something after all.

Well, that's pissing off your parents and finding what makes you happy in a nutshell! All the best out there and just remember — you don't need to join the army to be all that you can be... especially if someone who guts animals or gets naked is what you want to be!!!

Other Recommended Jobs

Activated Sludge
   Attendant
Aitchbone Breaker
Amalgamator
Amphibian Crew Member
Armhole Raiser
Asparagus Sorter
Ax Sharpener

Backside Grinder
Bait Packer
Balloon Dipper
Banana Ripening Room
   Supervisor
Barrel Bung Remover
Barrel Reamer
Bean Dumper
Beater
Beef Boner
Belly Builder
Belly Packer
Belter
Bender

Bin Filler
Biscuit Machine Operator
Bladder Changer
Blade Groover
Blanket Folder
Blaster
Bleacher, Lard
Blintze Roller
Blister Packing Machine
   Tender
Blow Off Worker
Blue Leather Sorter
Blunger Loader
Bobbin Salvager
Body Coverer
Boiler
Bologna Lacer
Bomb Loader
Bonbon Cream Warmer
Bone Crusher
Bosom Presser
Bottom Scrubber
Bowling Ball Weigher

Box Bender
Brain Picker
Brassiere Cup Mold Cutter
Breast Buffer
Breast Worker
Broom Handle Dipper
Buffer
Bung Driver
Bunghole Borer
Butter Melter
Butt Maker
Butt Presser

Cabbage Salter
Carcass Assembler
Car Spotter
Cat Chaser
Cat Hooker
Cathead Worker
Cereal Popper
Chicken Fancier
Clam Tonger
Cleat Thrower
Clocker
Cobbler
Coke Inspector
Container Filler
Cookie Breaker
Corker
Corn Popper
Cream Maker
Cutlet maker

Debeaker

Decal Applier
Detonator Assembler
Dice Maker
Double Bottom Driver
Dumper

Egg Breaker
Egg Smeller
Erector
Eyelet Row Market

Facial Operator
Fagoting Machine
    Operator
Family Dinner Service
    Specialist
Fig Washer
Fish Flipper
Fish Liver Sorter
Fish Sniffer
Fish Straightener
Frankfurter Assembler
Frog Shaker
Frothing Machine Operator
Fur Beater

Gang Leader
Gang Vibrator Operator
Germ Drier
Gimp Tacker
Gizzard Skin Operator
Glove Parts Inspector
Gravedigger
Grizzly Worker
Guillotine Operator

Gut Sorter
Gutter Mouth Cutter

Ham Hock Mopper
Handle Attacher
Hanger
Hardness Tester
Head Charrer
Helmet Hat Puncher
Hide Salter
Hog Head Singer
Horizontal Stick Turning
    Machine Operator
Hothouse Worker
Huckster
Human Projectile
Hummer Operator

Icing Spreader
Instant Powder Supervisor

Jigger
Jogger
Jockey Room Custodian
Jowl Trimmer
Jukebox Coin Collector

Kinker
Knober
Knocker-Off

Lap Checker
Leacher
Leg Skinner
Livestock Counter

Lozenge Maker Helper
Lubricator
Lump Inspector

Macaroni Press Operator
Masher
Mayonnaise Mixer
Mint Wafer Depositor
Mold Picker
Mother Tester
Mounter
Mucker

Nailer
Neverslip Stitcher
Nipple Machine Operator
Nougat Maker

Pad Attacher
Pan Greaser
Panty Hose Crotch Closing
    Machine Operator
Peanut Farmer
Pencil Inspector
Phone Book Deliverer
Pickler
Pie Topper
Pipe Smoker
Pocket Creaser
Powder Monkey
Puddler
Puffer
Pump and Blower
Puncher
Pure Culture Operator

Pusher
Putty Maker

Rabbit Dresser
Red Mold Thickener
Rib Bender
Ripper
River Crossing Supervisor
Road Hogger
Roustabout
Rug Stretcher

Salt Bellies Overhauler
Scorer
Scrubber
Sequins Stringer
Sewer Pipe Cleaner
Shackler
Shaft Sinker
Shovel Loader
Shrinker
Shuttlecock Assembler
Sign Hanger
Six Pack Packer
Slimer
Skoog Machine Operator
Sock Examiner
Smearer
Snagger
Spot Picker
Squeak, Rattle and Leak
    Repairer
Squirt Machine Operator
Stain Wiper

Steak Tenderizer
Stiff Leg Derrick Operator
Stiff Neck Loader
Stitch Fudger
Stogie Maker
Streaker
Stringer Up
Sublimer

Taffy Puller
Tea Leaf Reader
Tie Up Worker
Time Checker
Toe Puller
Toilet Attendant
Tooth Cutter
Towel Folder
Tree Surgeon
Tripe Cooker
Turkey Roll Maker

Upper Cutter

Vamp Wetter
Vein Pumper
Viscera Washer

Weed Inspector
White Kid Buffer
Wig Comber
Wood Piler
Wort Extractor
Wrinkle Chaser

Yarn Winder

Sources of Information

Department of Transportation (DOT) Dictionary of Occupational Titles Index, Information Technology Associates.

Greater New Haven Yellow Pages, SBC/SNET 2001.

Job Genie, www.stepfour.com/jobs/hrfree.htm, 74 Tremont Street, Hartford, CT 06105.

Powell, William, *The Anarchist Cookbook*, Fort Lee, New Jersey: Barricade Books, 1971, 1989.

The World's Tackiest Postcards, Palo Alto, California: Klutz Press, 1987.

The Official NASCAR Handbook, National Association of Stock Car Auto Racing, New York: HarperHorizon/Harper Collins Publishers Inc., 1998.

Fleischman, Bill and Pearce, Al, *The Unauthorized NASCAR Fan Guide '99*, Farmington Hills, Michigan: Visible Ink Press, 1999.

Boyle, James J., *Killer Cults*, New York: St. Martin's Press, 1995.

Bugliosi, Vincent, and Gentry, Curt, *Helter Skelter*, New York: Bantam Books, 1974.

Gross, Hawkeye K., *Drug Smuggling: The Forbidden Book*, Boulder, Colorado: Paladin Press, 1992.

Heidi Fleiss: *Hollywood Madam*, a Nick Broomfield film, New York: Fox Lorber Films, 1995.

Royal, Mickey, *The Pimp Game: An Instructional Guide*, Los Angeles: Sharif Publishing, 1998.

Loria, Ana, *Get Paid for Sex: The Big Bad Book of Sex Opportunities for Men and Women*, Malibu California, InfoNet Publications, 1999.

Loria, Ana, *1-2-3 Be a Porn Star!*, Malibu California, InfoNet Publications, 2000.

Tamidermy.Net, WASCO Manufacturing, Inc.

Bolles, Richard N., *What Color is Your Parachute? A Practical Manual for Job Hunters and Career Changers*, Berkeley, California, Ten Speed Press, 2002.

YOU WILL ALSO WANT TO READ:

☐ **40090 BEATING THE CHECK: How to Eat Out Without Paying,** *by Mick Shaw.* Pissed-off restaurant worker Mick Shaw lets fly at the restaurant industry in this heart-felt manual, and reveals all the techniques of *Beating the Check* he has learned in his years of low-paying wage slavery. A few schemes in the book include: when and where to attack; the simplest scams; how to leave without paying; and much, much more. *Beating the Check* is a book that can greatly reduce your food costs, plus it's fun, and you will have great stories to tell! *Sold for informational purposes only. 2000, 5½ x 8½, 72 pp, soft cover.* $8.00.

☐ **64245 FREELANCE WRITER'S HANDBOOK, Second Edition,** *by James Wilson.* Much has changed since the first edition, and technological advancements have led to this second edition. New developments include: faster computers, digital photography, e-mail, electronic submissions, and e-publishing, to name a few. Written by an author who has made his living writing 70 books and more than 1,000 magazine articles for over twenty years. He gives you the down-and-dirty facts about writing for money. Before you quit your day job, let an old pro show you how it's done. *2001, 5½ x 8½, 222 pp, soft cover.* $15.95.

JYM3

LOOMPANICS UNLIMITED
PO BOX 1197
PORT TOWNSEND, WA 98368

Please send me the books I have checked above. I am enclosing $_____ which includes $6.25 for First Class shipping and handling of orders up to $25.00. Please call for additional postage rates. *Washington residents please include 8.2% for sales tax.*

NAME _____

ADDRESS _____

CITY/STATE/ZIP _____

We accept Visa, Discover, and MasterCard. To place a credit card order *only,* call 1-800-380-2230, 24 hours a day, 7 days a week.
Check out our web site: www.loompanics.com

☐ **64129 SELL YOURSELF TO SCIENCE, The Complete Guide to Selling Your Organs, Body Fluids, Bodily Functions, and Being a Human Guinea Pig**, *by Jim Hogshire*. This book shows you exactly what your body is worth and how to sell it, in whole or in part. Your body is your business when you sell renewable resources such as blood, sperm, milk, and hair. You can also arrange to sell your heart, lungs, and other vital organs in the most unusual "going out of business" sale you've ever heard of. This amazing "career guide" also reveals what it's like to work as a guinea pig for drug companies. *1992, 5½ x 8½, 168 pp, illustrated, soft cover. $16.95.*

☐ **40093 THE REAL WORK, Essential Sleight of Hand for Street Operators**, *by Paul Price*. After becoming bored with creating illusions for children's birthday parties, Paul Price witnessed a game of Three Card Monte on the wharves of San Francisco. The following weekend, armed with his magician's knowledge of sleight of hand, our author threw away his magician's cloak and went to work on the streets. His first day netted him $200. After reading ***The Real Work***, you will no longer be among the mindless mass of followers. You will have the power to profit from the public's simple mindedness. Use it wisely. *Sold for entertainment and informational purposes only. 2001, 5½ x 8½, 80 pp, illustrated, soft cover. $12.00.*

JYM3

LOOMPANICS UNLIMITED
PO BOX 1197
PORT TOWNSEND, WA 98368

Please send me the books I have checked above. I am enclosing $_____ which includes $6.25 for First Class shipping and handling of orders up to $25.00. Please call for additional postage rates. *Washington residents please include 8.2% for sales tax.*

NAME_____

ADDRESS _____

CITY/STATE/ZIP _____

We accept Visa, Discover, and MasterCard. To place a credit card order *only,* call 1-800-380-2230, 24 hours a day, 7 days a week.
Check out our web site: www.loompanics.com

☐ **10065 HOW TO HIDE THINGS IN PUBLIC PLACES,** *by Dennis Fiery.* Did you ever want to hide something from prying eyes, yet were afraid to do so in your home? Now you can secrete your valuables away from home by following the eye-opening instructions contained in this book, which identifies many of the public cubbyholes and niches that can be safely employed for this purpose. Absolutely the finest book ever written on the techniques involved in hiding your possessions in public hiding spots. Illustrated with numerous photographs, an index of hiding places and appendices on Simplex lock combinations. *1996, 5½ x 8½, 220 pp, illustrated, soft cover.* $15.00.

☐ **10048 THE BIG BOOK OF SECRET HIDING PLACES,** *by Jack Luger.* This book tells how searchers find hidden contraband and how to hide your stuff so it can't be found. Topics include: hiding places in the home and the automobile; tools and techniques used by searchers; the different types of searchers you may encounter and the intensity of the searches they conduct; the tools you need to build your own secret hiding places and where to get them; how much work is involved; and much more. Whether you're hiding valuables, papers, prohibited items — or looking for them — this book is for you. *1987, 8½ x 11, 128 pp, more than 100 illustrations, soft cover.* $14.95.

JYM3

LOOMPANICS UNLIMITED
PO BOX 1197
PORT TOWNSEND, WA 98368

Please send me the books I have checked above. I am enclosing $_____ which includes $6.25 for First Class shipping and handling of orders up to $25.00. Please call for additional postage rates. *Washington residents please include 8.2% for sales tax.*

NAME _____

ADDRESS _____

CITY/STATE/ZIP _____

We accept Visa, Discover, and MasterCard. To place a credit card order *only,* call 1-800-380-2230, 24 hours a day, 7 days a week. Check out our web site: www.loompanics.com

☐ **13077 HOW TO MAKE CASH MONEY SELLING AT SWAP MEETS, FLEA MARKETS, ETC.,** *by Jordan L. Cooper.* You can make money selling at swap meets, flea markets, etc. — once in a while as a part-time income, or as a full-time business. After years of making good money at flea markets, the author lets you in on the secrets of success. His tips and how-to's were learned from the School of Hard Knocks and can save you some hard knocks of your own. Topics covered include: what to sell; how to display your wares; pricing; the IRS; and much, much more. A low initial investment is all that's required. You can still hold your regular job while getting started, and you will be your own boss. *1988, 5½ x 8½, 180 pp, illustrated, soft cover.* $16.95.

☐ **64167 SECOND-HAND SUCCESS: How to Turn Discards into Dollars,** *by Jordan L. Cooper.* This is the story of successful people who turn discards into dollars. Jordan L. Cooper reveals the tricks used by dozens of clever entrepreneurs to turn trash into treasures. Learn where to find all kinds of used merchandise and where to sell it for top dollar. From recycling to foraging in grandma's attic to making art from junk, this is the best resource of its kind. Topics covered include: sources of supplies; swap meet survival; used clothing; small appliances & household goods; seasonal merchandise; antiques & collectibles; arts & crafts from junque; handling problems; and much more! *1995, 5½ x 8½, 196 pp, illustrated, soft cover.* $14.95.

JYM3

LOOMPANICS UNLIMITED
PO BOX 1197
PORT TOWNSEND, WA 98368

Please send me the books I have checked above. I am enclosing $_____ which includes $6.25 for First Class shipping and handling of orders up to $25.00. Please call for additional postage rates. *Washington residents please include 8.2% for sales tax.*

NAME_____

ADDRESS _____

CITY/STATE/ZIP _____

We accept Visa, Discover, and MasterCard. To place a credit card order *only,* call 1-800-380-2230, 24 hours a day, 7 days a week.
Check out our web site: www.loompanics.com

☐ **64145 $HADOW MERCHANT$, Successful Retailing Without a Storefront,** *by Jordan L. Cooper.* How to make money in low-overhead, street corner-style operations by someone who's been there. Covers: swap meets; flea markets; street corners; arts & crafts shows; mall kiosks; fairs & carnivals; gun shows; special interest events; and much more! Also includes valuable advice on pitfalls to avoid. Shadow businesses are highly mobile, low-cost, low-risk operations that can be started without giving up your regular job. Many of the world's most famous businesses started out this way. The next success story could be yours. *1993, 5½ x 8½, 152 pp, illustrated, soft cover. $12.95.*

☐ **64210 THE TEMP WORKER'S GUIDE TO SELF-FULFILLMENT, How to slack off, achieve your dreams, and get paid for it!,** *by Dennis Fiery.* Temporary employment, or "temp work," can be a treasure trove of opportunity for the dedicated practitioner. Rather than being a series of dead-end meaningless short-term jobs, temp work offers numerous advantages. This book explains how to effectively exploit and undermine the temp system. It contains all the information needed to successfully obtain steady, lucrative work as a temp, while satisfying the requirements of the employers who are seeking competent temp workers and fulfilling your own special needs. *1997, 5½ x 8½, 152 pp, illustrated, soft cover. $12.95.*

JYM3

LOOMPANICS UNLIMITED
PO BOX 1197
PORT TOWNSEND, WA 98368

Please send me the books I have checked above. I am enclosing $_____ which includes $6.25 for First Class shipping and handling of orders up to $25.00. Please call for additional postage rates. *Washington residents please include 8.2% for sales tax.*

NAME _____

ADDRESS _____

CITY/STATE/ZIP _____

We accept Visa, Discover, and MasterCard. To place a credit card order *only,* call 1-800-380-2230, 24 hours a day, 7 days a week.
Check out our web site: www.loompanics.com

☐ **64240 MAKE $$$ AS A NON-FICTION WRITER,** *by Duncan Long.* You want to write, but how do you break into the field? Author and educator, Duncan Long, who has over 30 years experience as a non-fiction writer shows you the ropes. Find out if you have the right stuff to become a writer; What are realistic expectations of income as a writer; Do you have to use an agent; Is freelancing your only option; What kind of workspace and equipment do you need; How do you find those elusive writing assignments. If you've been wanting to make writing your full- or part-time career, don't put it off any longer. Let Duncan Long show you how to get started today. *2000, 5½ x 8½, 219 pp, soft cover.* $14.95.

☐ **14193 BACKYARD MEAT PRODUCTION,** *by Anita Evangelista.* If you're tired of paying ever-soaring meat prices, and worried about unhealthy food additives and shoddy butchering techniques, then you should start raising small meat-producing animals at home! You needn't live in the country, as most urban areas allow for this practice. This book clearly explains how to raise rabbits, chickens, quail, ducks, and mini-goats and -pigs for their meat and by-products, which can not only be consumed but can also be sold or bartered to specialized markets. Improve your diet while saving money and becoming more self-sufficient! *1997, 5½ x 8½, 136 pp, illustrated, soft cover.* $14.95.

JYM3

LOOMPANICS UNLIMITED
PO BOX 1197
PORT TOWNSEND, WA 98368

Please send me the books I have checked above. I am enclosing $_____ which includes $6.25 for First Class shipping and handling of orders up to $25.00. Please call for additional postage rates. *Washington residents please include 8.2% for sales tax.*

NAME_____

ADDRESS _____

CITY/STATE/ZIP _____

We accept Visa, Discover, and MasterCard. To place a credit card order *only,* call 1-800-380-2230, 24 hours a day, 7 days a week.
Check out our web site: www.loompanics.com

☐ **14175 SELF-SUFFICIENCY GARDENING, Financial, Physical and Emotional Security From Your Own Backyard,** *by Martin P. Waterman.* A practical guide to organic gardening techniques that will enable anyone to grow vegetables, fruits, nuts, herbs, medicines and other useful products, thereby increasing self-sufficiency and enhancing the quality of life. Includes sections on edible landscaping; greenhouses; hydroponics and computer gardening (including the Internet); seed saving and propagation; preserving and storing crops; and much more, including fact-filled appendices. The author is a highly regarded journalist and gardener, world-recognized fruit breeder and is a director of the North American Fruit Explorers. *1995, 8½ x 11, 128 pp, illustrated, indexed, soft cover.* $13.95.

☐ **14099 THE ART & SCIENCE OF DUMPSTER DIVING,** *by John Hoffman.* This book will show you how to get just about *anything* you want or need — food, clothing, furniture, building materials, entertainment, luxury goods, tools, toys — you name it — *ABSOLUTELY FREE!* Take a guided tour of America's back alleys where amazing wealth is carelessly discarded. Hoffman will show you where to find the good stuff, how to rescue it and how to use it. You'll find illustrated techniques, recipes for salvaged food, how to convert trash to cash, and how to handle run-ins with cops. It took the author a life time to learn this — all it takes for you is this book. *1993, 8½ x 11, 152 pp, illustrated, soft cover.* $14.95.

JYM3

LOOMPANICS UNLIMITED
PO BOX 1197
PORT TOWNSEND, WA 98368

Please send me the books I have checked above. I am enclosing $_____ which includes $6.25 for First Class shipping and handling of orders up to $25.00. Please call for additional postage rates. *Washington residents please include 8.2% for sales tax.*

NAME _____

ADDRESS _____

CITY/STATE/ZIP _____

We accept Visa, Discover, and MasterCard. To place a credit card order *only,* call 1-800-380-2230, 24 hours a day, 7 days a week.
Check out our web site: www.loompanics.com

☐ **85225 A MAN'S GUIDE TO ADVERTISING FOR A WOMAN, How to Find the Woman of Your Dreams Using the "Personals" Section of Newspapers, Magazines and the Internet,** *by Sebastian Phillips.* Men! Are you desperately seeking a woman... or would you like to? Then this book is a must! It explains how to properly structure "Personals" ads that will attract not *one*, but *many* women. Learn where, when and why to place your ads, buzzwords that get results, the do's and don'ts of composition, how to screen your responses, and how to stack the odds in your favor so that the war between the sexes comes to a screeching halt and love and courtship prevail! Contains never-before-published information on Internet ads, as well as informed details on magazines and newspaper advertising. This is the best book ever written on this subject. *1996, 5½ x 8½, 184 pp, illustrated, soft cover.* $16.95.

☐ **40084 HOW TO SNEAK INTO THE MOVIES,** *by Dan Zamudio.* Why let Hollywood bigwigs, bad actors, and cowardly studio executives rip you off? The author has worked in several movie theaters and reveals all his tricks for sneaking into the movies, including the four basic ways to get into the movies free. Highlighted with true tales of sneaking into some of America's great movie palaces. If you are tired of being milked for box office duds, then lower your cost of movie-going — and your risk of getting caught — by learning exactly *How to Sneak Into the Movies!* Contents include: How to sneak in with a date without her thinking you're cheap; what to do when you're caught; and more. *1995, 5½ x 8½, 64 pp, soft cover.* $8.00.

JYM3

LOOMPANICS UNLIMITED
PO BOX 1197
PORT TOWNSEND, WA 98368

Please send me the books I have checked above. I am enclosing $_____ which includes $6.25 for First Class shipping and handling of orders up to $25.00. Please call for additional postage rates. *Washington residents please include 8.2% for sales tax.*

NAME_____

ADDRESS _____

CITY/STATE/ZIP _____

We accept Visa, Discover, and MasterCard. To place a credit card order *only,* call 1-800-380-2230, 24 hours a day, 7 days a week.
Check out our web site: www.loompanics.com

☐ **58148 MODERN FRAUDS AND CON GAMES,** *by Tony Lesce.* Fraud is the fastest growing industry in the world, which is why it's becoming a global trillion-dollar problem. The main reason is that it's low-risk compared to other crimes. Overall, the apprehension rate is about three percent and the conviction rate is about one percent. This volume describes dozens of frauds, many of which are not even illegal, but do involve deception for economic gain. It sheds light on the new frauds and con games, with an extensive chapter on steps you can take to reduce your vulnerability to fraud. No book on fraud can be the final word, but this will help you protect yourself and your family. *2002, 5½ x 8½, 178 pp, soft cover.* $15.00.

☐ **40095 DON'T BE A VICTIM!, How to Protect Yourself from Hoaxes, Scams, and Frauds,** *by Michael E. Chesbro.* Hoaxes, scams, frauds… tens of thousands of people become victims of these crimes every year. But how can so many people be conned out of their life savings, be tricked into paying for products and services they will never receive, or even lose their complete identity to these criminals? This book looks at various different hoaxes, scams, and types of fraud. We will learn to recognize these crimes for what they are and we will look at things we can do to protect ourselves from becoming victims of these crimes. It is important to remember, however, that no book can identify every possible hoax, scam, or fraud every variation of these crimes. There will always be some new twist, some new way that criminals find to take advantage of the unsuspecting. What we can do is learn to recognize the most common of these crimes, and to recognize the underlying principles that make these crimes successful. *2002, 5½ x 8½, 143 pp, soft cover.* $12.95.

JYM3

LOOMPANICS UNLIMITED
PO BOX 1197
PORT TOWNSEND, WA 98368

Please send me the books I have checked above. I am enclosing $_____ which includes $6.25 for First Class shipping and handling of orders up to $25.00. Please call for additional postage rates. *Washington residents please include 8.2% for sales tax.*

NAME _____

ADDRESS _____

CITY/STATE/ZIP _____

We accept Visa, Discover, and MasterCard. To place a credit card order *only,* call 1-800-380-2230, 24 hours a day, 7 days a week. Check out our web site: www.loompanics.com

☐ **58136 COPS! Media vs. Reality,** *by Tony Lesce.* Police officers are ever-popular subjects in the media. We see cop shows on TV, including both fictional detectives and reality-based shows such as *Cops,* in which TV crews accompany police officers on patrol, raids, and other activities. Police are also one of the hottest news items on radio and TV news programs. Each year brings a new crop of cop movies from Hollywood. Each year sees many crime novels appear, often written by people with an incomplete knowledge of their subject. There are many differences in the way law enforcement appears in the media, and the way it really is. This book will explore the reasons why, and present a picture of the way law enforcement really operates. It will highlight the contrasts between the ways cops are portrayed on TV and in the movies, and the way they work in real life. It will show why news reporting, which is supposed to be accurate and factual, often is not. *2000, 5½ x 8½, soft cover.* $13.95.

☐ **40050 MAKING CRIME PAY,** *by Harold S. Long.* What does it take to succeed at a criminal activity? What does it take to make crime pay? Written by a professional criminal, this book delves deeply into the realities of the criminal justice system and offers many hard-won suggestions for successfully evading the law. It is packed with information not available anywhere else. It explains what makes some criminals successful while others get caught. It also discusses how to deal with police, courts, and the criminal justice system to minimize apprehension and conviction. *1988, 5½ x 8½, 78 pp, soft cover.* $9.95.

JYM3

LOOMPANICS UNLIMITED
PO BOX 1197
PORT TOWNSEND, WA 98368

Please send me the books I have checked above. I am enclosing $_____ which includes $6.25 for First Class shipping and handling of orders up to $25.00. Please call for additional postage rates. *Washington residents please include 8.2% for sales tax.*

NAME_____

ADDRESS _____

CITY/STATE/ZIP _____

We accept Visa, Discover, and MasterCard. To place a credit card order *only,* call 1-800-380-2230, 24 hours a day, 7 days a week.
Check out our web site: www.loompanics.com

☐ **58143 LAST SUPPERS, Famous Final Meals from Death Row,** *by Ty Treadwell & Michelle Vernon.* How's this for a last meal: 24 tacos, 2 cheeseburgers, 2 whole onions, 5 jalapeño peppers, 6 enchiladas, 6 tostadas, one quart of milk and one chocolate milkshake? That's what David Castillo, convicted murderer, packed in the night before Texas shot him up with a lethal injection. Execution rituals have always varied slightly from state to state, not only in the method of death but also in the care and treatment of the accused during his final hours. One ritual that remains constant throughout all 38 states which have the death penalty is the act of feeding the condemned man a special last meal before the execution. The quantity and quality of the food available to the inmate does vary, but prisoners are always allowed to partake of one final feast before they shake hands with the Grim Reaper. *2001, 8½ x 5½, 146 pp, soft cover.* $14.95.

☐ **19209 OUT OF BUSINESS, Force a Company, Business or Store to Close It's Doors... for Good!,** *by Dennis Fiery. Sometimes playing by the rules isn't good enough.* When filing a formal complaint, asking for your money back, and engaging in healthy competition just don't do the trick, you need to take serious action. This book arms you with 101 ways to derail, deflate, and destroy your target business. And if you want to protect your own business, this book is the best insurance policy you'll ever buy. Author Dennis Fiery gives new meaning to the term "corporate downsizing" in this revenge treatise. Don't get mad. Don't get even. Get revenge. *Sold for informational and entertainment purposes only. 1999, 5½ x 8½, 290 pp, soft cover.* $17.95.

JYM3

LOOMPANICS UNLIMITED
PO BOX 1197
PORT TOWNSEND, WA 98368

Please send me the books I have checked above. I am enclosing $_____ which includes $6.25 for First Class shipping and handling of orders up to $25.00. Please call for additional postage rates. *Washington residents please include 8.2% for sales tax.*

NAME _____

ADDRESS _____

CITY/STATE/ZIP _____

We accept Visa, Discover, and MasterCard. To place a credit card order *only,* call 1-800-380-2230, 24 hours a day, 7 days a week. Check out our web site: www.loompanics.com

☐ **85293 DRINK AS MUCH AS YOU WANT AND LIVE LONGER, The Intelligent Person's Guide to Healthy Drinking,** *by Frederick M. Beyerlein.* Seems anything you do these days is an overture to trouble. Can't smoke or your lungs become festering cancer depots. Can't eat your favorite good or your arteries turn into solid lead. Can't indulge in recreational drugs without some macho DEA officer banging down your door. But there is one thing left. You can drink. Yes, booze. Hooch. Spirits. And you can drink as much of it as you want. With Nutritionist Frederick M. Beyerlein's system, you'll never get a hangover again. Reading this book is the best thing you can do for your body. *1999, 5½ x 8½, 209 pp, illustrated, indexed, soft cover.* $14.95.

☐ **85299 GOURMET CANNABIS COOKERY, The High Art of Marijuana Cuisine,** *By Dan D. Lyon.* Why settle for the same old pot brownies from a mix when you can whip up an entire gourmet marijuana meal — from starters to dessert — in your own kitchen? Author Dan D. Lyon makes cooking with pot easy, fun, and delicious. Step-by-step instructions explain how to cultivate your own herb for recipes, how to modify commercial mixes and how to serve up menus that will keep your friends buzzing for hours. Why eat rather than smoke? Dan D. Lyon tells readers that it's more economical, healthier, and safer. *1999, 5½ x 8½, 90 pp, illustrated, soft cover.* $10.00.

JYM3

LOOMPANICS UNLIMITED
PO BOX 1197
PORT TOWNSEND, WA 98368

Please send me the books I have checked above. I am enclosing $_____ which includes $6.25 for First Class shipping and handling of orders up to $25.00. Please call for additional postage rates. *Washington residents please include 8.2% for sales tax.*

NAME_____

ADDRESS _____

CITY/STATE/ZIP _____

We accept Visa, Discover, and MasterCard. To place a credit card order *only*, call 1-800-380-2230, 24 hours a day, 7 days a week.
Check out our web site: www.loompanics.com

☐ **11119 SURVIVING ON THE STREETS, How to Go DOWN Without Going OUT,** *by Ace Backwords.* Street people! We see them frequently in our day-to-day travels, but we don't have a clue as to how they survive on the streets. We may get brief glimpses into their world, the missions, the ragged individuals asking for spare change, the soup kitchens, but Ace Backwords gives us our first real foray into daily life on the streets. Intended to be written as a how-to for anyone contemplating or more likely thrust by circumstances into street life, it is an uncensored and candid look at an entirely different world that exists codependently to the one with which most of us are familiar. This book offers specific tips on street survival that worked and some that didn't, a brutally honest peek into an alien world from the eyes of a native. *Fascinating! 2001, 8½ x 11, 196 pp, illustrated, soft cover.* $14.95.

☐ **19197 STREET SMARTS FOR THE NEW MILLENNIUM,** *by Jack Luger.* Being street smart can mean the difference between being safe or becoming a victim in today's dangerous society. There are criminal elements and pitfalls in everyday life that pose real risks for the average citizen. **Street Smarts for the New Millennium** explains how to: develop a street smart attitude and heightened awareness; depend on personal resources instead of police; avoid dangerous situations; protect yourself, your family; your assets and your health; enhance your personal safety; improve your job security; and much more. Don't fall prey to muggings, carjackings, rapes, and other street crimes! Learn to be self-reliant! Read this book and develop your **Street Smarts for the New Millennium**! *1996, 5½ x 8½, 134 pp, soft cover.* $15.00.

JYM3

LOOMPANICS UNLIMITED
PO BOX 1197
PORT TOWNSEND, WA 98368

Please send me the books I have checked above. I am enclosing $_____ which includes $6.25 for First Class shipping and handling of orders up to $25.00. Please call for additional postage rates. *Washington residents please include 8.2% for sales tax.*

NAME _____

ADDRESS _____

CITY/STATE/ZIP _____

We accept Visa, Discover, and MasterCard. To place a credit card order *only*, call 1-800-380-2230, 24 hours a day, 7 days a week.
Check out our web site: www.loompanics.com

☐ **88173 DON'T LET THEM PSYCH YOU OUT!,** *by George Zgourides, Psy. D.,* This is one of the finest psychological self-defense manuals we have seen. *Difficult people.* We all know some. The noisy (or nosy) neighbor, the over-bearing boss, the relentless relative, the pushy salesperson. *Manipulative people.* People who insist on having everything their way. People who are always trying to *psych you out!* We all know them, but do we know how to deal with them? ***Don't Let Them Psych You Out!*** can help. It teaches psychological self-defense for handling arguments, showdowns, ambushes, and other difficult situations. This book won't help these conflicts go away. But it will give you practical skills for handling difficult people without losing your dignity or your cool. *1993, 5½ x 8½, 198 pp, soft cover.* $15.95.

☐ **64225 CHEATING AT BLACKJACK SQUARED, The Dark Side of Gambling,** *by Dustin D. Marks.* This unique book represents the definitive resource on how professional con men cheat at Blackjack and other card games. The author, a former high-stakes cheater, explains an amazing array of specific moves with clear, understandable text and detailed, easy-to-understand illustrations. Obtain a once-in-a-lifetime view inside the hidden, dark world of cheating where the stakes are high (and not only in terms of money), the most innocuous gesture becomes a signal, and the playing cards are tools of deception. *1996, 6½ x 8½, 201 pp, illustrated, indexed, soft cover.* $24.95.

JYM3

LOOMPANICS UNLIMITED
PO BOX 1197
PORT TOWNSEND, WA 98368

Please send me the books I have checked above. I am enclosing $_____ which includes $6.25 for First Class shipping and handling of orders up to $25.00. Please call for additional postage rates. *Washington residents please include 8.2% for sales tax.*

NAME_____

ADDRESS _____

CITY/STATE/ZIP _____

We accept Visa, Discover, and MasterCard. To place a credit card order *only,* call 1-800-380-2230, 24 hours a day, 7 days a week.
Check out our web site: www.loompanics.com

3534

☐ **64227 SMART CASINO GAMBLING, How to Win More and Lose Less**, *by Olaf Vancura, Ph.D.* Written for anyone who even thinks about stepping into a casino. *Smart Casino Gambling* is a fast-paced yet down-to-earth guide that will improve every player's chances of winning more (or maybe losing less). In an anecdotally rich fashion, Dr. Vancura leads the reader through an entertaining and educational tour of each of the most popular casino games. Included are numerous excerpts from interviews with gaming leaders and industry executives representing major casinos around the country. This book will explain which games can legitimately be beaten, and which to avoid if you want to keep your shirt. In a light-hearted yet factual way, he teaches you how casinos *really* make their billions, including the tricks used to part players from their money. 1996, 6½ x 8½, 334 pp, illustrated, indexed, soft cover. $24.95.

☐ **88888 2003 LOOMPANICS MAIN CATALOG,** *8½ x 11, 279 pp, soft cover.* $5.00. You will receive our catalog *Free* when you order any of the titles above. If you would like to order just the catalog, the cost is $5.00

You can send us your order with payment enclosed, or check out our web site at www.loompanics.com. If you are ordering with a credit card (Visa, MasterCard, or Discover) you can order online at the above web site or you can call our toll-free order desk at 1-800-380-2230, 24 hours a day, 7 days a week, or fax us your order at 1-360-385-7785.

JYM3

LOOMPANICS UNLIMITED
PO BOX 1197
PORT TOWNSEND, WA 98368

Please send me the books I have checked above. I am enclosing $_____ which includes $6.25 for First Class shipping and handling of orders up to $25.00. Please call for additional postage rates. *Washington residents please include 8.2% for sales tax.*

NAME _____

ADDRESS _____

CITY/STATE/ZIP _____

We accept Visa, Discover, and MasterCard. To place a credit card order *only*, call 1-800-380-2230, 24 hours a day, 7 days a week.
Check out our web site: www.loompanics.com

The Best Book Catalog In The World!!

We offer hard-to-find books on the world's most unusual subjects. Here are a few of the topics covered IN DEPTH in our exciting new catalog:

Hiding/Concealment of physical objects! A complete section of the best books ever written on hiding things.

Fake ID/Alternate Identities! The most comprehensive selection of books on this little-known subject ever offered for sale! You have to see it to believe it!

Investigative/Undercover methods and techniques! Professional secrets known only to a few, now revealed to you to use! Actual police manuals on shadowing and surveillance!

And much, much, more, including Locks and Lock Picking, Self-Defense, Intelligence Increase, Life Extension, Money-Making Opportunities, Human Oddities, Exotic Weapons, Sex, Drugs, Anarchism, and more!

Our book catalog is over 260 pages, 8½ x 11, packed with more than 800 of the most controversial and unusual books ever printed! You can order every book listed! Periodic supplements keep you posted on the LATEST titles available!!! Our catalog is **$5.00,** including shipping and handling.

Our book catalog is truly THE BEST BOOK CATALOG IN THE WORLD! Order yours today. You will be very pleased, we know.

LOOMPANICS UNLIMITED
PO BOX 1197
PORT TOWNSEND, WA 98368

Name _____

Address _____

City/State/Zip _____

We accept Visa, Discover, and MasterCard. For credit card orders *only,* call 1-800-380-2230, 24 hours a day, 7 days a week.
Check out our Web site: www.loompanics.com